WARY MEYERS' TOSSED & FOUND

WARY MEYERS'
TOSSED & FOUND

UNCONVENTIONAL DESIGN FROM CAST-OFFS

Linda & John Meyers

Stewart, Tabori & Chang
New York

Published in 2009 by Stewart, Tabori & Chang
An imprint of Harry N. Abrams, Inc.

Library of Congress Cataloging-in-Publication Data:
Meyers, Linda, date
Wary Meyers' Tossed and found / by Linda and John Meyers.
p. cm.
ISBN 978-1-58479-808-8
1. Handicraft. 2. Found objects (Art) 3. House furnishings. I. Meyers,
John, 1966- II. Title.
TT157.M472 2009
745.5--dc22
2009001534

Editor: Dervla Kelly
Book Designed by Linda Meyers, with Gary French
Production Manager: Tina Cameron

The text of this book was composed in Bernhard Antique and Plantin.

Printed and bound in China
10 9 8 7 6 5 4 3 2 1

HNA
harry n. abrams, inc.
a subsidiary of La Martinière Groupe
115 West 18th Street
New York, NY 10011
www.hnabooks.com

To Booberry

with many thanks...

Sean Mewshaw, for his savoir faire in trigonometry, carpentry, and film directing. Without him the Picnic Table and Eiffel Mantel would forever remain just pencil drawings.

Courtenay Kendall, for championing us to *Time Out New York* magazine.

Time Out New York magazine, for their enthusiasm, and for never editing any of our projects.

Our agent **Sarah Jane Freymann,** for sending that first email entitled "Ever thought about a book?"

Our editor **Dervla Kelly,** along with the outstanding team at Stewart, Tabori and Chang.

And to our parents:
Anne and John Wary, for giving Linda a youth filled with weekend yard sales and flea markets;

Kathie and Peter Meyers, for showing John the value of never throwing anything out (against all intentions to do otherwise . . .).

projects

YARD
SALE

SAT - SUN

800 - 300

seating

tables

storage

lighting

decorative

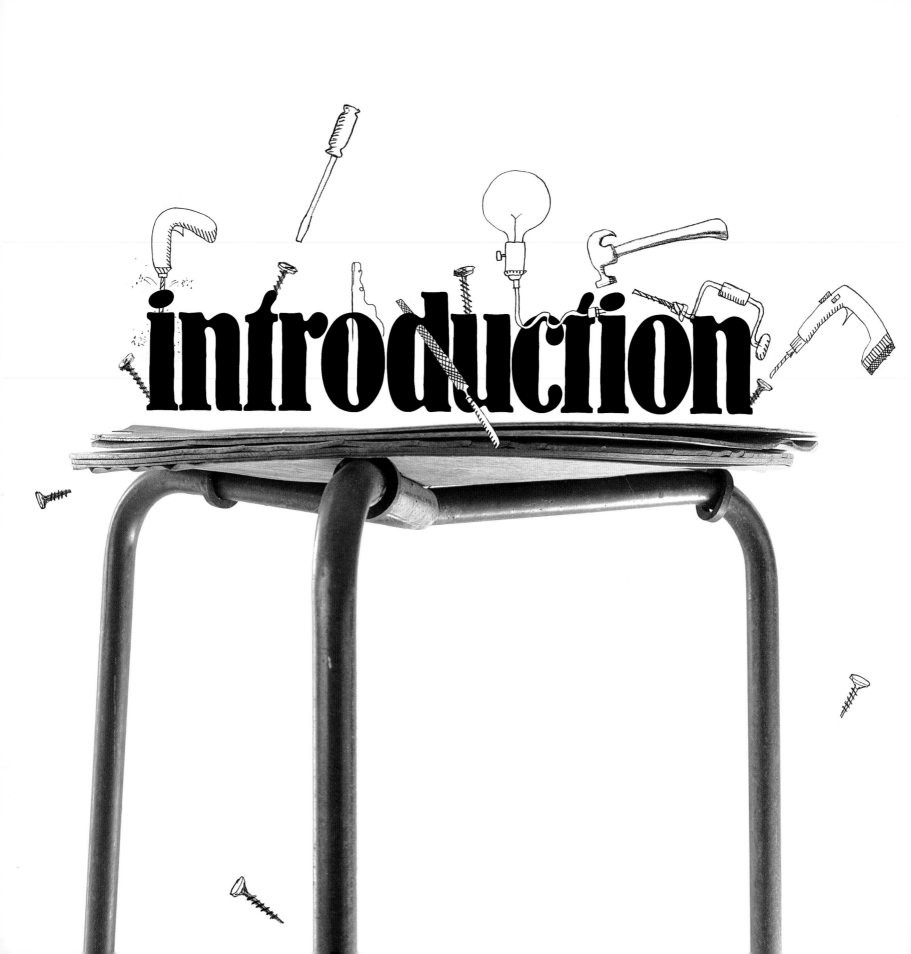

introduction

In the fall of 2006, *Time Out New York* magazine asked us to write an article about refurbishing cast-off housewares from the streets of New York City. With apartment living space a precious commodity, the NYC sidewalks are a common dumping ground for things that don't fit, don't work, or are perfectly good. Our assignment for the article was to fix the ones that didn't work, for instance gluing a cracked tabletop or stitching a seam back together. We wrote down sanitation truck schedules, drove around, and found a plethora of abandoned furnishings, and got to work. At the time of the article we had just finished the interiors of two apartments in New York. Both had to be stylish, but use limited funds, since in New York (and anywhere for that matter) budgets can be blown on a single couch. Our resourceful reuse and repurposing of items landed us the *Time Out* job. Because anything goes when working with furniture that's been tossed aside, the article ended up being a bit more eccentric than expected. It turned into a biweekly column for a year, and at the end, we donated all the items we'd made to charity.

Both Linda and I have a history of bringing things home from yard sales, flea markets, thrift stores, and the side of the road. There is no rhyme or reason to what we collect, other than we like it, it looks good, and it prevents waste. We furnished our entire apartment this way, with new things rescued from certain doom every week. But in time, much like the New Yorkers we wrote about, we had a basement full great stuff, but were limited on living space. Luckily there were friends who needed their apartments

decorated, and this is how we started our business. In 2004, Linda and I moved to Maine, got married, and formed Wary Meyers Decorative Arts. Linda came from a background as a graphic designer and art director in New York City, and I was the Corporate Display Director for Anthropologie. Initially setting up shop to paint portraits and design clothing, we found ourselves constantly on the road back to New York, designing interiors. Fortunately, we acquired clients that wanted the Bohemian aesthetic we had, so it was just a matter of going to more yard sales, flea markets, and thrift stores, which we did every weekend anyway.

As an incidental of all this yard saling and driving around, we ended up with a bunch of things that would be great in some other incarnation, like a ton of barn wood, a bunch of bent plywood, a bolt of chintz, a pile of Astroturf, and a set of pastry bags. This was all fantastic stuff that you would probably not think to go shopping for, therefore definitely should not end up in the landfill. So, we thought we'd make something of our proverbial basement full of surplus raw material.

The intention of the book is to let people know there are creative, economical, and ecofriendly alternatives to buying a new dresser, chair, or even iPod speakers. This book is set up with full instructions, and although we realize some of the projects may be a bit out-there, we hope the essential qualities of them will act as inspiration. For instance, you may not want to make a picnic table as intense as ours (page 68), but you might notice how great the wood looks and be inspired to go find some

old planks and put them across a pair of sawhorses. Or if you don't want to make the stuffed jean quilt letters (page 186) you can just stitch denim together to make your own boro. With these uncomplicated alterations you don't have to buy a new table and you'll have a blanket to lovingly repair for decades. On the other hand some projects are so simple that you may want to expand on them. If you chose to, the 1x2" molding project (page 156), as seen in the concept sketches, could become as complicated as a trigonometric formula written in longhand Cyrillic and nailed to your wall in 3-D. On the other hand, you may just want to paint a stripe across a canoe instead of drawing a blue willow design (page 86). All the projects can be used as a jumping-off point, much like their original incarnations from yard sales, bulk trash pickup days, thrift stores, or the side of the road.

We are not expert carpenters or electricians, so if you're a beginner, fear not—the projects are designed so that anyone can make them, usually with just the tools you have around the house. Up until last year we were using a hand coping saw instead of an electric jigsaw, and only recently bought an electric palm sander at a yard sale for the Wingback Plywood Chair (page 16). The projects are also prototypes, so there may be something we did out of order, or there may be a better way to achieve the end result; our afterthoughts are mentioned in the instructions. The materials are something else, as we know that not everybody may find an old pharmacy funnel, or a pipe organ, but whatever you substitute, the tenets of economy, resourcefulness, and creativity remain the same.

seating

Every day, all types of would-be seating are put out to pasture, so there's no shortage of goods available if you're interested in exercising your creativity. This is not to say that all chairs that appear on the sidewalk or in a yard sale are in need of alteration or customization, but sometimes they are, or perhaps you'll find a bit of one or a piece of another. There's a chance you'll see something in a store like a stool or chair and see that it's the perfect blank canvas (Engraved Aalto Stool, page 30; Blue Willow chair, page 24). Just be sure it has a decent base that doesn't need to be changed. For example, the Pool Noodle Chair (page 54) is just a new structure attached to a solid iron base, as is the Wingback Plywood Chair (page 16) and to some extent, the Skeleton Chair (page 46). Adding to an untouched foundation in this manner usually assures you don't overwork it. It's nice to see the balance of the original item and its additions. This idea is taken to the extreme with the The Visible Chair (page 36), where an entire old chair fits inside an entirely new chair. The exception here is the Chaise-burger (page 40), whose "decent base" was clouds of white poly fill.

wingback plywood chair

This chair is built from three different pieces—an unknown type of wood, a basic utilitarian vinyl chair, and a steel-and-plastic auditorium chair. All of it was headed for the landfill during a springtime bulky trash pickup week. Whereas there were plenty of perfectly good complete chairs also looking at the same fate, it's nice to be able to make something completely new.

The frame is from a Steelcase Max Stacker, the common plastic lobby waiting-room chair. We picked it up with the intention of carving the back like a Chippendale splat. Although this time there wasn't enough height to pull it off, anything could have been carved out of the plastic (monogram, a cipher, a logo, a pattern, a pineapple, etc.). Charles and Ray Eames punched a small heart out of the back of one of their own bent plywood designs of a child's chair and a church in Eastern Bohemia cut crosses from their plastic chairs. The possibilities are endless.

The back of our wooden chair is a mystery; we found it tucked into a bin with some old life preservers (which we kept to make stuffed animals), so it may

have been part of a boat. Whatever it was, it makes a distinctive "winged" back, and a modern take on the traditional 18th-century wingback chair, which was made to protect the sitter from the blasting heat of a roaring fire. The seat is from an old basic vinyl chair, stripped of its vinyl, dried-out foam, and endless staples. All the parts needed refinishing. The chrome came clean easily with steel wool, however the seat needed hours of sanding, and the back needed a new faux finish since the plywood was so weathered. The faux wood grain was surprisingly simple to achieve, so don't let that stop you from attempting this project. The only problem you may have is bending plywood, or finding an abandoned skateboard ramp as a substitute. If neither of these sounds realistic at least you can get some ideas of how to Frankenstein your own chair. The aim is to be creative, not waste, and have fun.

OPPOSITE, LEFT TO RIGHT: Another angle; the steel frame; the seat being sanded.
CLOCKWISE FROM BOTTOM: Smoothing the back and seat with palm sander; ripping out the vinyl piping of the seat; raw materials; the finished product.

tools & supplies

- vinyl chair
- pliers
- wood filler (optional)
- palm sander
- sandpaper (60-, 100-, 200-grit)
- nutmeg-colored gel stain
- Max Stacker
- steel wool (optional)
- hacksaw
- plywood (bent)
- white oil-based primer (optional)
- paintbrush
- gloves
- rags
- ½" rubber insulated clamps with rubber gasket linings

step 1

To make the seat: remove the vinyl, foam, and staples from the seat piece of the vinyl chair. If the staple holes are too big, you'll need to fill them with stainable wood filler. If there is adhesive on the seat, it will come off in sanding. Sand the entire seat, front and back. We used a palm sander, but soon found that due to the ghosting of old oxidation, we needed to really rasp the surface with 60-grit sandpaper and elbow grease. After the 60 grit, use 100, then finish with a smoother 200 grit. Stain with a coat of gel stain.

step 2

To make the chrome frame: take off the plastic back and seat of the Max Stacker and either recycle them or set them aside. For the wire frame, use .0000 grade steel wool to remove all the dirt, dullness, pitting, and rust. Small pieces are best, so just pull off a little steel wool from the bundle. There is a thick piece of chair frame that must be removed since it's in the way of the new seat, and unfortunately it's the biggest piece, so you'll need some energy to saw through the steel. Use a hacksaw with a new blade.

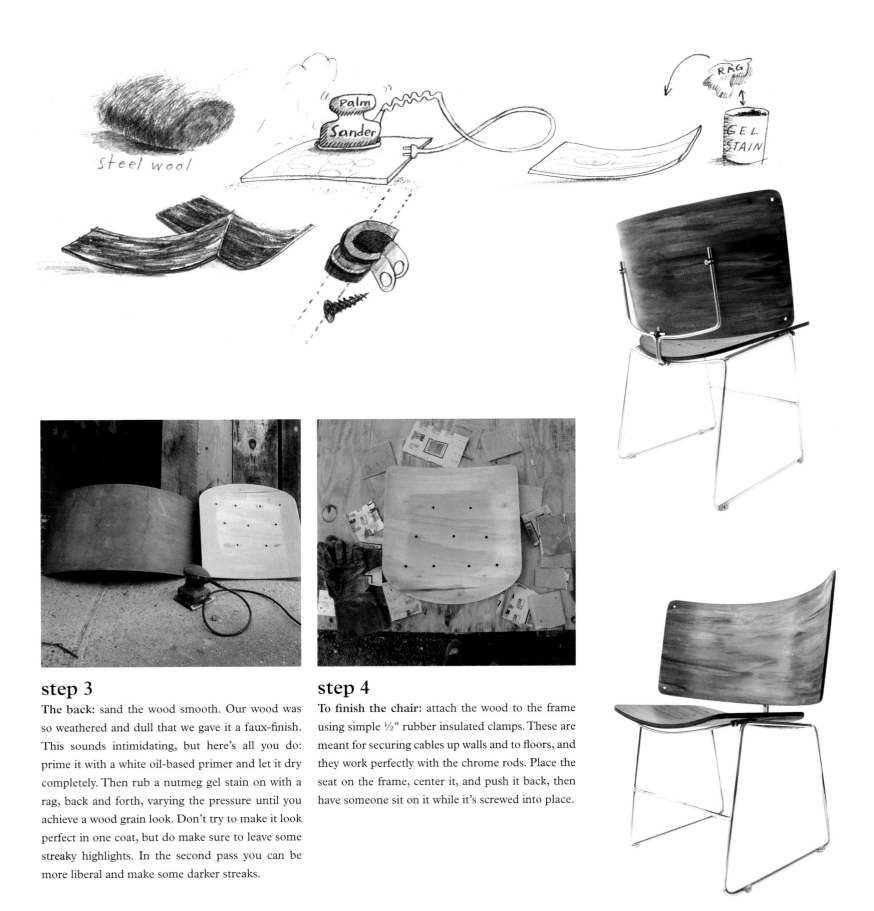

step 3

The back: sand the wood smooth. Our wood was so weathered and dull that we gave it a faux-finish. This sounds intimidating, but here's all you do: prime it with a white oil-based primer and let it dry completely. Then rub a nutmeg gel stain on with a rag, back and forth, varying the pressure until you achieve a wood grain look. Don't try to make it look perfect in one coat, but do make sure to leave some streaky highlights. In the second pass you can be more liberal and make some darker streaks.

step 4

To finish the chair: attach the wood to the frame using simple ½" rubber insulated clamps. These are meant for securing cables up walls and to floors, and they work perfectly with the chrome rods. Place the seat on the frame, center it, and push it back, then have someone sit on it while it's screwed into place.

golden drip

This idea came about when it was time to say goodbye to our fan-back wicker chair that had weathered a few harsh Maine winters on our porch. The first idea was to cut something into the back, like a Chinese Chippendale design, or a cipher like the Monogrammed Key (page 192), or cut away the wicker leaving just a back design. We also considered making a skeleton back, or something like the Initialed Rug (page 166). But we decided against those in favor of an upholstered look. One of the first ideas was an upholstered Chippendale splat design, but the sketch (next page) looked like a drip or a type of pour. The next sketches solidified—or rather liquefied—that idea. We would make a big drippy upholstered antimacassar. At first we wanted to sew it out of nice worn leather, and have it look like it was antique, but in this crazy shape, like something out of an Jules Verne novel. But there was no way we'd find the leather. Gold seemed like a natural. This type of wicker chair is meant for a light-filled room anyway, so it was off to the fabric store. We found the metallic gold faux-leather in the dance fabrics area.

We sketched many drip shapes onto muslin, sewed them almost closed, and stuffed them before finalizing these particular designs. We can tell you that a fauteuil only looks good dripping all the way down, and the seat needs the accompanying "footeuil," the molten gold "kiss," sliding to the floor.

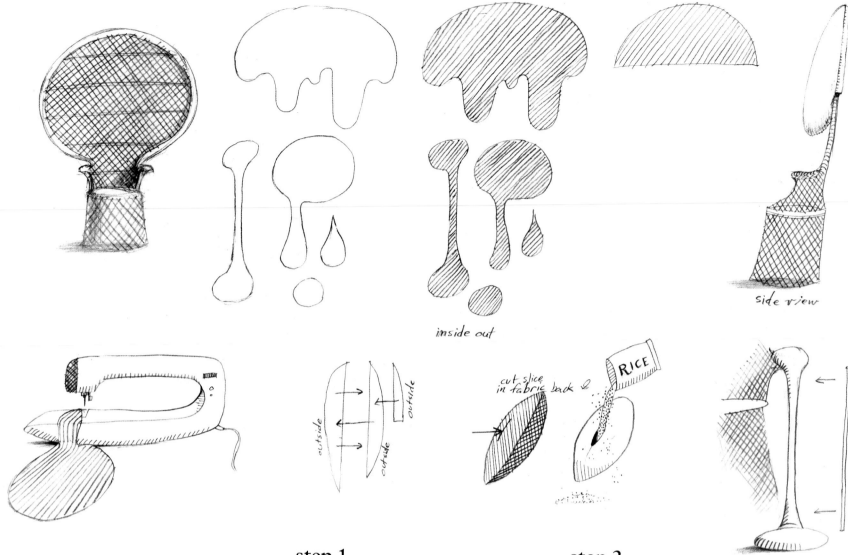

inside out

side view

outside outside outside outside

cut slice in fabric back &

RICE

tools & supplies

- muslin
- stick of charcoal
- scissors
- sewing machine
- poly fill
- about 20 pounds
  uncooked rice
- gold fabric
- ½x36" dowel
- needle and thread

step 1

You'll want to make all of these pieces in muslin first, to make sure they look right since wicker chairs differ slightly. Place a piece of muslin across the back, and charcoal the back edge, so you have that big curve as a guide. Draw the drips where they look good, but don't make the upper curve between two drips too sharp, or puckering will occur.

step 2

You will be cutting a double thickness of muslin (and stuffing like a pillow), so lay the marked muslin on top of another piece. To compensate for the stuffing, and to help it slide over the top easier, cut the entire shape about 2" wide on each side plus an additional ½" seam allowance. Sew the double thickness together almost all the way around, leaving an opening to turn it inside out. Sew the semicircle, which is the sleeve for the top, to the back piece of the top, as in diagram (either one could be the back). Turn them inside out and stuff them with rice and poly fill. Just a little rice is needed to accentuate the drip and keep it laying against the wicker; if it were just poly fill it wouldn't look like it's dripping. Do this for all the shapes until they fall right and look drippy.

CLOCKWISE FROM TOP LEFT: Muslin tracing the chair; conceptual sketches; shapes ready to be cut out

chesterfield   art macassar

step 3

Now lay down a double thickness of the gold fabric with right sides together and trace the muslin shapes. Remember to allow an extra 2" on each side for the filling, and ½" seam allowance. Cut out the gold pieces, turn them inside out, and stitch them closed. Remember to attach the semicircle sleeve to the back of the top drip. Once the shapes are sewn you'll need to cut a slit in the back of them—this is difficult because of the double thickness. Make sure you don't cut through both layers! The cut should be made in the center of the back in order to stuff it easily. This is where the poly fill and the rice will be poured in and sewn up afterwards.

step 4

Pour in the rice and stuff with some poly fill. There's no real measurement; you just need to eyeball it— when it looks like it's dripping it's ready. The sleeve of the top back should fit over the curve of the back. There will be some natural wrinkles across the front, due to the convex curve of the wicker. The long drip from the fauteuil requires an armature. Use a length of ½" wooden dowel. There should also be rice most of the way up this drip, and poly fill near the top, and then rice again on the fauteuil.

step 5

When everything is in place you may want to stitch the seat cushion to the chair—the weight of the rice drip could send it over the edge. Also a stitch on the fauteuil and a couple on the back pocket will keep the front from falling forward (use gold metallic thread for this, just in case it's visible through the wicker). Otherwise everything pretty much stays in place because of the rice.

blue willow chair

We had this old Eames chair in our basement, and even though its avocado green upholstery had seen its salad days, we just couldn't throw it out. Nor could we reupholster it, given the way it was constructed. We figured the fabric was sufficiently like a canvas, and taut enough to not crack the latex paint when someone sat in it. So on the heels of painting the Blue Willow Canoe (page 86), we turned our brushes to the chair.

The willow pattern we designed for the chair is based on Thomas Minton's original Orientalist motif that he engraved for Spode in 1780. It includes a story of two young lovers being chased by the emperor (her father) on the bridge, and the getaway boat in the water. The Japanese-style clouds in the sky replace the two doves that the lovers turned into after they died in a fire started by the emperor. The border pattern is a thickened "net-work" (referring to Chinese fishing nets), the pagodas are graphic interpretations of the pagodas and pattern ideas sketched out on pages 28-29, and the tree behind the left temple owes its leaf shape to the English designer Celia Birtwell. We chose blue willow because we love the pattern, but it seemed

a little unexpected on a mid-century chair, much like a modern fabric would look on a Louis XIV chair. It is this odd juxtapositioning of old against new, handmade against machine made, which makes things interesting and unique—a balanced design when you're working with found and worn things. As another example, we took the photo opposite when we were just about finished—the only thing left to do was paint the legs white. But after we painted them the chair just did not look good at all; it seemed that we had gone too far and it was overproduced. There were three components to the chair: the seat, shell, and legs. The perfect balance would have been to change just one thing.

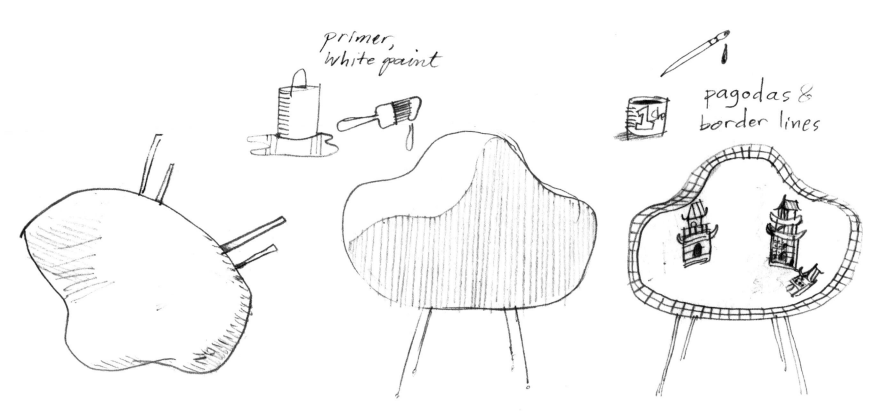

primer, white paint

pagodas & border lines

tools & supplies

- chair
- white latex primer paint
- brushes
- white latex paint
- blue enamel paint
- charcoal

step 1

First vacuum the upholstery, and clean it as best you can. Ideally you would paint a fiberglass Herman Miller chair, not a fabric one, but had we found a fiberglass chair, we probably would never have done this.

Paint the fabric with white latex primer and make sure to cover every little space, but don't be heavy handed—put on just enough to cover the upholstery. After the primer has dried, paint the fabric with white latex paint.

step 2

Now using the blue enamel, paint the borderlines and the pagodas. If you do it in steps like this it'll be easier and you'll be sure to complete it all. If you're hesitant to jump right in with a paint brush, lightly sketch the lines on first with a stick of charcoal and paint over them. The lines should be about 1" apart, and have 1"-wide segments. Next paint three pagodas, you can see some examples on the following pages. Paint one large palace in the upper right, one smaller house in the lower right, and another large palace in the upper left.

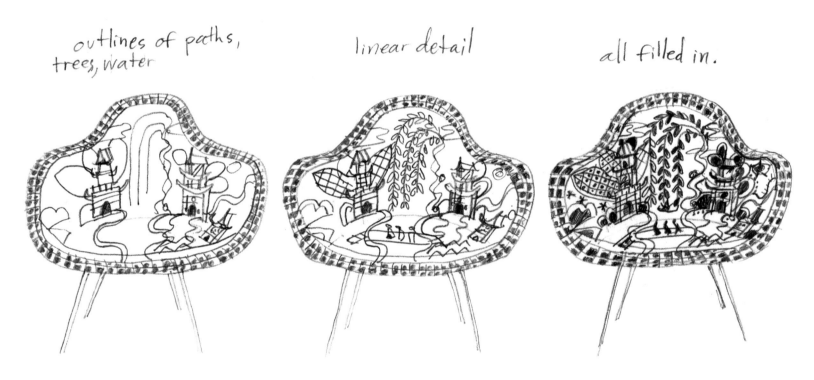

outlines of paths, trees, water

linear detail

all filled in.

step 3

Now paint the outlines of the paths, trees, and water. The willow tree in the middle is crooked and burly. The orange tree to the right is really just some stylized round bushes on a trunk, and the tree behind the left pagoda is really an overgrown rhododendron. The paths are curvy, and have two line borders. The fence in the lower right is a series of parallelograms.

step 4

Fill in the solid squares in the border, and crisscrosses in the trees. Draw the bridge with three figures on it, the willow leaves, outlines on bushes, random decorative elements such as round graphics, stars made of lines, and the little man in the boat.

step 5

Fill in everything else. The willow leaves, the dots in the rhododendrons, the orange tree leaves, bushes, the fence, and perhaps put a little wavy line in the water.

engraved aalto stool

Alvar Aalto, often called the father of Modernism, was a Finnish architect and designer. In 1932 he designed this stackable "60 stool." The stool with its bent plywood legs was a triumph of functional modernism, or functionalism. Legend has it that Aalto hurled the prototype stools across his workshop for testing, when one finally withstood the test, he said "That's the one! We'll sell thousands!" Of course he sold millions, which brings us to the project at hand. Target sells a knockoff of the 60 stool, and that's what we started with. Patinas take a long time to acquire, but make just about everything look more organic, mellow, and appealing. Shiny plastic and shearling are two exceptions. But luckily the knockoff stools are wood, and our project makes them look like we've had them for years. Beyond just a honeyed, golden aging to them, they should have a history of marks. This doesn't mean banging them with chains and hammers and sanding off a coat of fresh paint—that result will always look artificial. But doing it right—patiently and with a hands-on approach—we wanted a patina on our stools that might fool even Tom Dixon. A sense of humor is important too, so we looked to Alice Cooper's

classic album "School's Out" for the inspiration. The album cover is a photo of a school desk, engraved and carved and looking almost exactly like the stool top opposite. We used household items to distress the surface and changed the initials AC to AA. If you don't want to copy Alice Cooper, we've printed a spread from our old patinated notebook on pages 34 and 35 with some type ideas, including a feather, dagger, box cutter, and an Aalto stool typeface.

THIS PAGE:
Distressed Finnish

tools & supplies

- stool
- sandpapers (60- and 100-grit)
- block
- pocket plane
- box cutter
- claw hammer
- needle file
- pencil
- nutmeg gel stain
- rags
- red food coloring

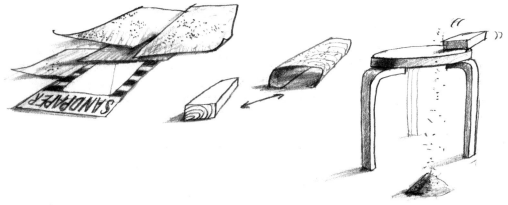

step 1

The stool may come with a light polyurethane finish on it that you'll need to remove with sandpaper. (You'll put a finish back on them at the end.) Wrap the sandpaper in a block to make it easier. You can also use the edges of the block to put slight v-shaped cuts into the edges of the stool. Don't go overboard, but concentrate the wear on the areas that would normally be damaged over the years, i.e., the bottom of the legs, the curves of the legs, and the edge of the seat.

step 2

Using a pocket plane, chip away at the veneer top of the stool. This will make some sections of veneer peel away. Slice into these areas with a box cutter to make a straight peel (see main photo). The scrapes on the legs, in addition to the sanding block marks, were made by raking the claw hammer across the wood. The claw hammer also accounts for the "softer" marks on top. The names and initial were carved with the box cutter and finished with a needle file to dull the sharp edges of the blade.

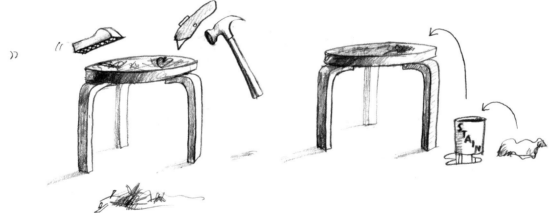

step 3

Draw the heart "tattoo" on with pencil. Originally this said "School's Out" and "Alice Cooper." We changed it to "Stool's Out" and "Wary Meyers." You could write anything though. After it's penciled, take the box cutter and needle file to it. There is another area toward the bottom that originally had the Warner Bros. logo. We changed it to a Wary Meyers logo. A feather might look good here (see next page for simple ideas).

step 4

After all the sanding and carving is done it's time to stain it (we used a nutmeg gel stain). Stain the entire stool with a rag, wiping it off as you do, and try to get it deep into the cracks, new marks, initials, and peeled veneer. The large heart gets stained with red food coloring. Repeat the staining if necessary, or sand it a little more in some spots, then stain it again. Treat this like finger painting. Let stools dry for at least a week before using, to make sure the stain is totally dry.

ABCDEFGHIJKLM or M
NOPQRST UVWXYZ
or

1234567890

LINDA 2009 LINDA

ABCDEFGHIJ
KLMW

John + Linda

LMW

wary meyers

wary meyers

wary meyers

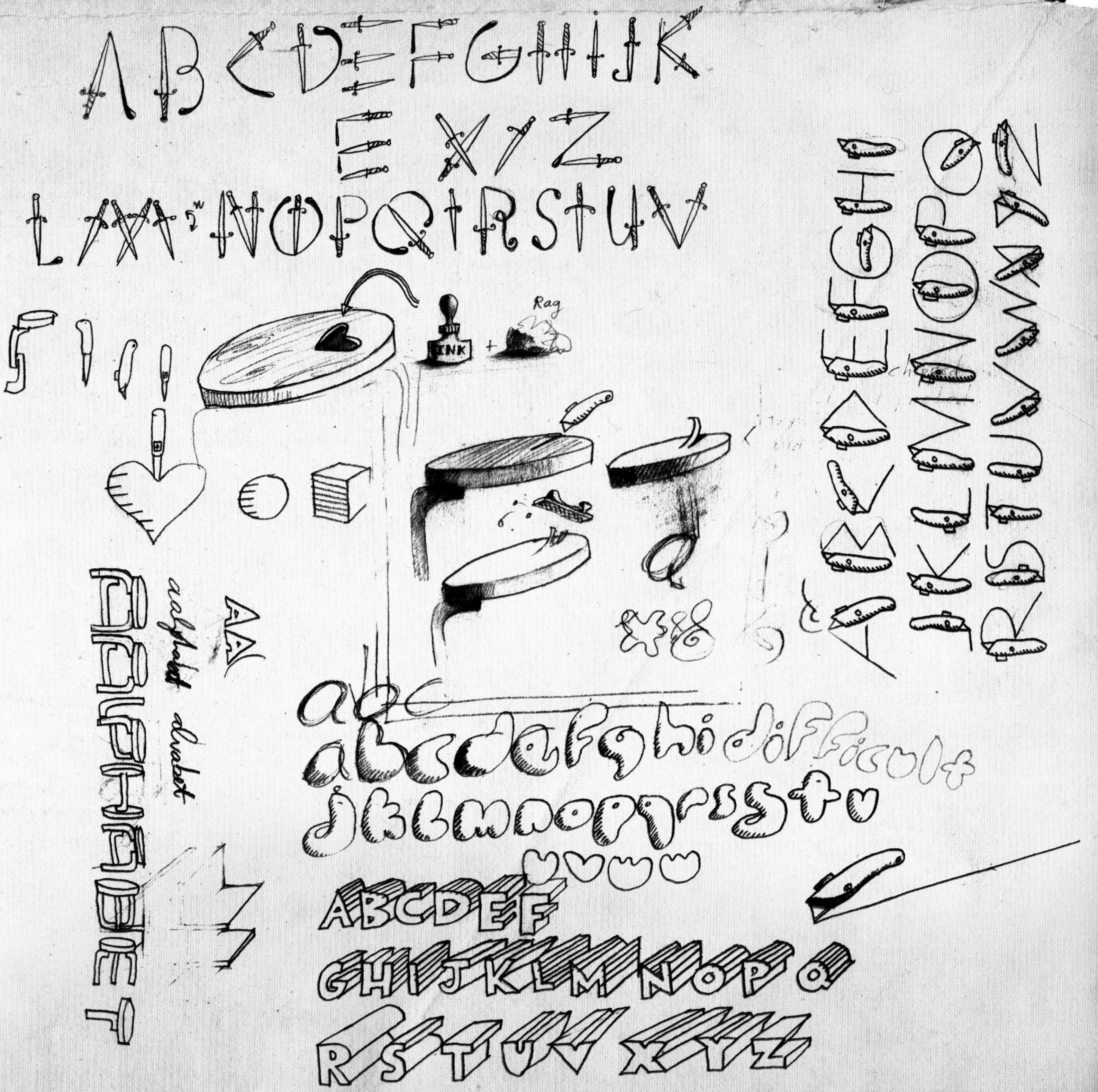

A B C D E F G H I J K

E X Y Z

L M N O P Q R S T U V

Rag
INK +

AA
alphabet

ALPHABET

abc
abcdefghijklmn opqrsstu

ABCDEF
GHIJKLMNOP Q
RSTUVXYZ

ABCDEFGHI
JKLMNOPQ
RSTUVWXYZ

the visible chair

One day we stopped at an estate sale, where, in a heap in the basement, we found two old Chippendale chairs with cabriole lion's paw legs. Everything about them was well thought out, nicely designed, and beautiful. Even a little rough around the edges, they looked like they should be in a museum.

Chippendales are, in our opinion, the most perfect chair to design with. Combining the past with the present (old with new, organic with technological, etc.) is one of the great themes of the aesthetic world. With that balance concept in mind, there was a myriad of things we could do, but it seemed like every one of them involved touching or altering the chairs. The museum idea led to a do-not-touch idea. Museums have great ways of showing things off (see Art Base, page 144). So, like a museum might do, we decided to encase one of the chairs in Lucite. At first the idea was just to make a Lucite box to enclose it, possibly with a short white base on the bottom. While this may have looked good, pragmatically it would have

been awkward. If you take away the basic idea of a chair, you take away the design and become an anti-designer. Wouldn't it be best if the Lucite were functional as well? It would be there to protect, but also to enhance—to codesign. To that end, the Lucite box was dropped down in front to follow, in stark

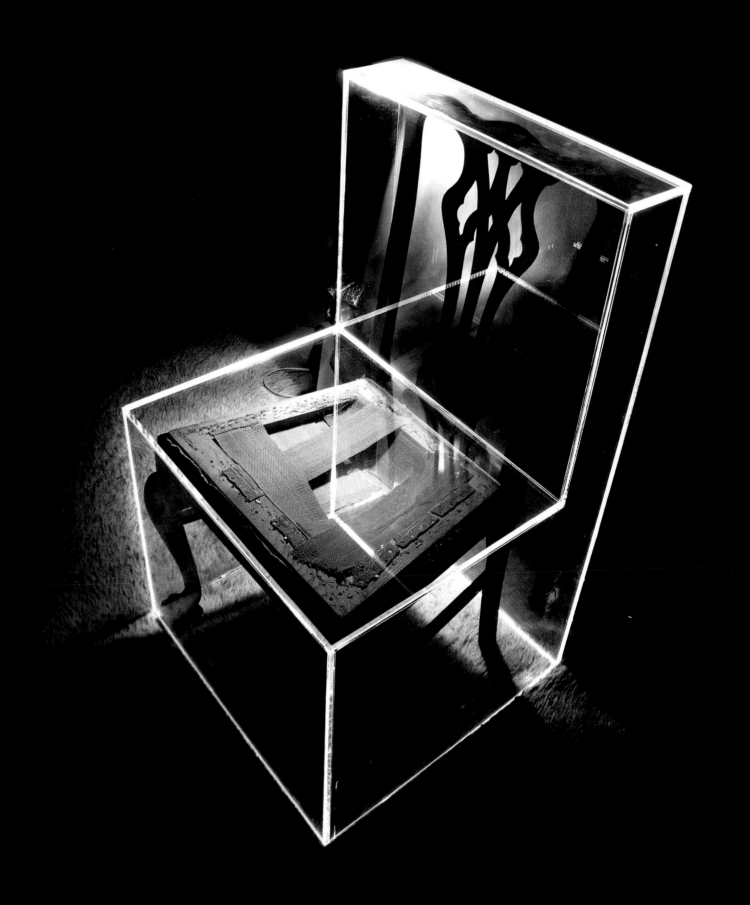

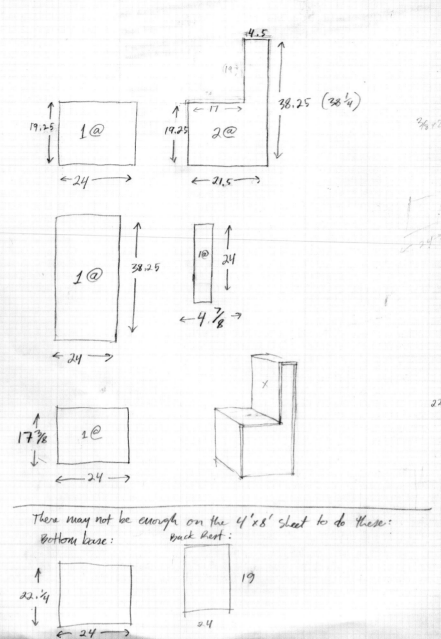

geometry, the lines of the Chippendale. By doing that, the Lucite case now became a chair; a Donald Juddian slipcover. We measured the Chippendale and designed the Lucite box to fit ½" away from the chair at its closest point. So now we had two chairs—one beautifully turned hand-carved antique and one sleek, modern, "glass box," looking like a self-contained museum exhibit of the history of the chair. Or like a see-through plastic anatomy model, "The Visible Chair." We had the Lucite cut, polished, and glued by professional plastic fabricators from ⅜" thick Lucite, following the plans provided. Of course all chairs differ so you'll have to draw up your own plans.

- chair
- 4x8' sheet ⅜" Lucite

chaise-burger

Two all satin patties, special sauce, bacon, cheese, pickles, onion in a sesame seed bun.

This is a folly of satin whimsy Linda cooked up for lounging in her closet. All the ingredients—including the sesame seeds—can be knocked over and sprawled around for a smorgasbord of relaxation.

Linda's had a fascination with fake food for some time, and she'd always thought of making some type of larger-than-life soft sculpture. When we came across colossal amounts of poly fill at an estate sale, she felt something huge was in order. We thought about mushrooms and snails (not in the food sense, rather more for scale), but their connotations might be too psychedelic, given what Linda's closet looked like already. Another idea was a large Formica box, the size of a sofa, filled with giant stuffed satin donuts, all removable, in all flavors including jelly. However the cheeseburger image was very pop and filled with color, and the idea that it could be taken apart and put back together again, to order, was definitely appealing. We thought also of a giant wrapper printed with our logo and a piece of stuffed cheese attached with Velcro, like "cheese paper" (we may still do this). Like the dozen donuts idea, it seemed like a perfect kids' room "chair"—something that could be jumped onto like a big pile of raked up autumn leaves. (For that matter, imagine a giant heap of hundreds of stuffed satin leaves!) We also thought about putting straps on the special sauce so it could be worn as a cape, and expanding the bacon to blanket size. In the end, though, it comes off as more of a closet fantasy for a grown-up.

There were some satin colors that weren't available at the fabric store, namely tomato red, lettuce green, and cheese yellow. We ended up using swimsuit Lycra for the cheese, but held the lettuce and tomato. The curled bacon is formed with pipe cleaners, which Linda braided and stitched into the edges. An ingredient breakdown is on the following pages. Bon appétit!

RIGHT: Chaise-burger
at home in Linda's closet

tools & supplies

- fabric (see list)
- One 34"x100 yd. bolt
  of batting
- poly fill, roughly seven
  32 oz bags
- about twenty four
  2-foot-long pipe cleaners
- ¼"-thick high-density
  poly foam
- sewing machine
- needle & thread (colors
  to match materials)
- Velcro

sesame seeds: ecru satin— 30 at approximately 4x3"

top bun: tan satin— 1 at 34"d, ecru satin— 1 at 32"d

bacon: brown-red satin— 4 at 39x12", ecru satin— 4 at 39x12"

cheese: yellow satin or spandex Lycra— 2 at 28x28"

burger: brown satin— 2 at 32"d

pickle: green satin— 4 at 15"d

special sauce: coral satin— 2 at 36"d (amoebic shaped)

onion: white satin— 2 at 32"d, lavender satin— 1 at 10x100"

cheese: yellow satin or spandex Lycra— 2 at 28x28"

burger: brown satin— 2 at 32"d

bottom bun: tan satin— 1 at 32"d, ecru satin— 1 at 32"d

step 1

To make the top bun: cut one 34" diameter circle of tan satin: this will be the top of the top bun. Now cut one 32" diameter circle ecru satin: this will be the bottom of the top bun. With the right sides together (the dull finish on the outside) sew the top bun pieces together with a ¼" seam allowance. The top is bigger, but only by 2 inches, so you can cheat that by gathering the top fabric a little bit at a time around the circumference, but of course no more than a total of 2". This is an "eyeballing" way of "ease" stitching.

Once these are together, cut a small hand-size slit in the middle of the ecru (bottom) piece, and turn the fabric inside out, so the satin finish is on the outside. Stuff the floppy bun with poly fill, until it looks like the photo. Hand stitch the slit closed with ecru-colored thread.

step 2

To make the bacon: cut a double thickness of the red-brown satin 39x12" and slice into four long pieces, two being 4", and two being 2". Repeat with the remaining two pieces of red-brown satin. Make the ecru strips the same way. Arrange as in the illustration, stitching the "meats" (red-brown) to the "fats" (ecru). You should have four striped bacon pieces: two tops and two bottoms.

Sandwich a piece of ½" flat batting between the top and bottom of the bacon (nice sides on outside) and stitch this closed—don't bother stitching this inside out, as the edges of bacon are a little more raw anyway, and the pipe cleaners still need to be put in.

Find the biggest pipe cleaners you can, and braid them together into a 39" length. Be sure to cover the raw pipe cleaner wire ends in tape before stitching them into the edge of the bacon, or else they may poke through. We twisted together about six pipe cleaners for each edge, so we ended up with twelve little annoying wire ends. Fold the bacon edges around the pipe cleaners and sew closed. Fold the raw ends of the bacon into a clean edge and stitch closed.

step 3

To make two slices of cheese: on a double thickness of fabric cut two 28" square pieces of yellow fabric. Turn the two nicer sides toward each other, and stitch together, with the usual ¼" seam allowance. Turn inside out and insert a piece of ¼"-thick high-density poly foam (you'll find this at the fabric store in the foam area—it comes in all thicknesses, and its main purpose is for upholstery). Stitch cheese closed with yellow thread. Repeat to make the second piece of cheese.

step 4

To make two burgers: on a double thickness of brown satin, cut two 32" diameter circles. With the right sides together (the dull finish on the outside), sew two pieces together with a ¼" seam allowance. Cut a hand-sized slit in the back of one, turn right side out, and stuff with poly fill. If it's a little lumpy that's fine—it looks more like a burger that way. Stitch slit closed with brown thread. Repeat for the other burger.

step 5

To make two pickles: on double thickness of green satin, cut two 15" diameter circles. Sew two pieces together like the burger, but insert ½" batting instead of poly fill. Close with green thread. Repeat for the other pickle.

step 6

To make the onion: on a double thickness of white satin, cut two 32" diameter circles. Sew together like the burger. Turn inside out, but do not stuff yet. To make the onion edge: cut a double thickness of lavender satin 10x100". Sew the lavender strip like the burger, but don't stuff it. Sew the lavender onto the white edge of the unstuffed onion. Stuff the whole thing conservatively, for this needs to look flat, or as thick as and even with the edge.

step 7

To make fifteen sesame seeds: on a double thickness of ecru satin, cut fifteen 4" sesame seed shapes. Sew two pieces together like the burger, but not all the way closed. Here it's easier and cleaner looking to leave a bit of stitching edge unsewn and stuff the poly fill in from there. Repeat for the rest of the seeds. Cut small lengths of adhesive-backed Velcro, and stick either half onto the sesame seeds. Save the remaining halves for the top bun.

step 8

To make the special sauce: cut a double thickness of the coral satin into a 36" diameter rounded star shape. Stitch like the burger, and fill with batting, stuffing a bit more into the "points" of the star.

step 9

To make the bottom bun: cut one 32" diameter ecru circle and one 32" diameter tan circle. The tan piece goes on the bottom. Sew like the burger, but stuff with a 2" piece of high-density poly foam, along with a topping of batting to fill out the edges.

step 10

Randomly stick the reserved halves of the Velcro to the top bun and attach the sesame seeds. Assemble the Chaise-burger as shown. Enjoy!

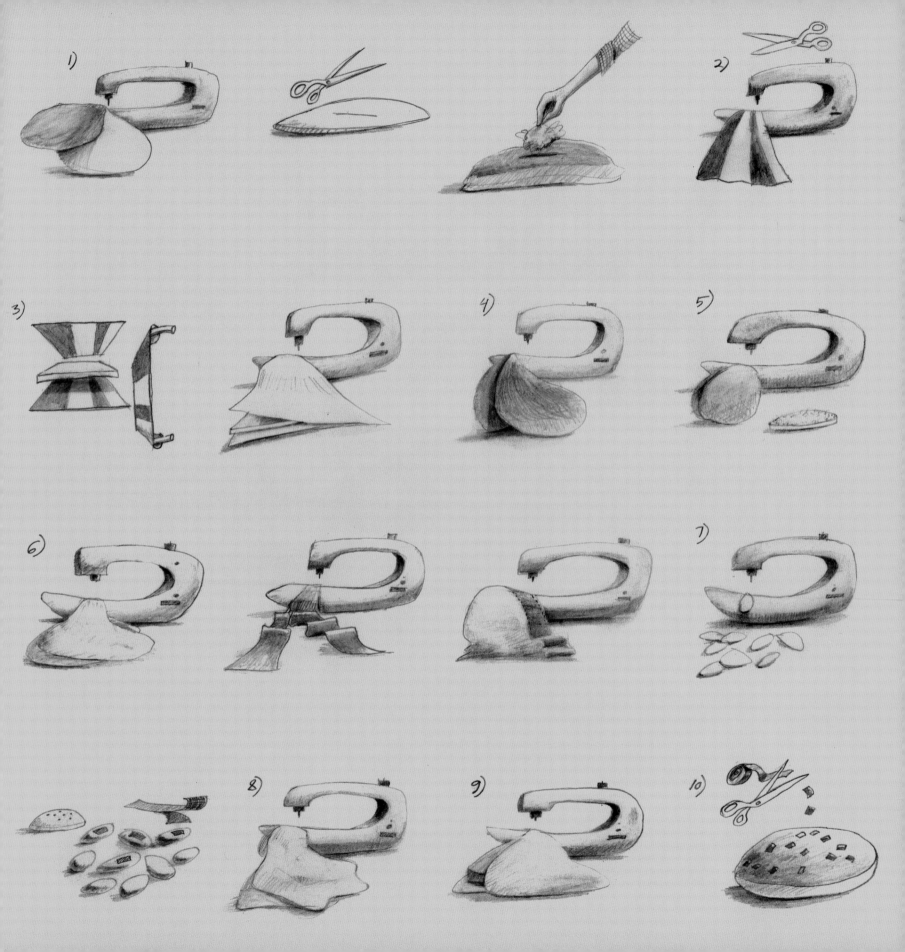

skeleton chairs

Thomas Chippendale was an 18th-century English furniture maker and the author of *The Gentleman and Cabinet-Maker's Director: Being a Large Collection of the Most Elegant and Useful Designs of Household Furniture in the Gothic, Chinese, and Modern Taste"* (exactly the subtitle we wanted for this book). He also designed the chair style known as "Chippendale," with a bowed back rail and a pierced splat back.

Chippendale chairs are the quintessential "antique" chair, and as such, lend themselves nicely for some "old vs. new" work. In this case, we use "ribbon-back" Chippendales (a variation with 4 strips of carved mahogany across the back instead of the traditional splat). We found them on the side of the street in Manhattan, missing their seats and a couple of ribbons. The splat back is an ideal design for experimenting with and redesigning, so we set to drawing out some concepts. We thought about where exactly our spine would hit the chair back, which quickly turned into the thorax splat idea. We drew it out on plywood and cut it out with a hand-held battery-operated jigsaw, although nowadays I highly recommend using a scroll saw. I also suggest using solid wood, not plywood, and cutting with the grain of the wood vertically, not horizontally.

The seats were missing, so we cut plywood shapes to match, and with batting and a traditional fabric we rebuilt the seats. The chairs are old and pieces were pegged in rather than screwed in; it was refreshing to put the splats into the chairs in a truly handmade way, like a surgeon.

I think this idea looks really great, and probably would look even better on a Chippendale with Cabriole-style turned front legs ending in lion's paw feet, like some salmagundi from the office of Dr. Moreau.

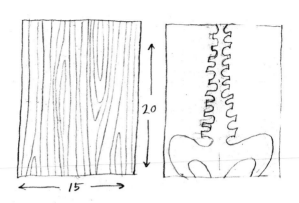 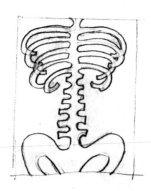 

tools & supplies

- wood
- charcoal stick
- drill and bits
- scroll saw
- sandpaper
- ⅜" wooden dowel
- rubber mallet
- wood glue (optional)
- wood stain

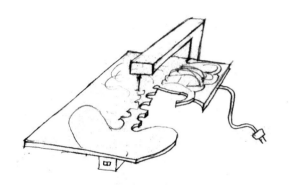 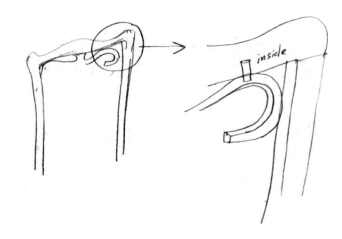

  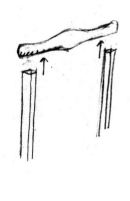 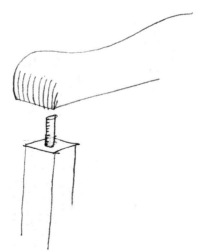 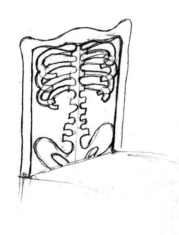

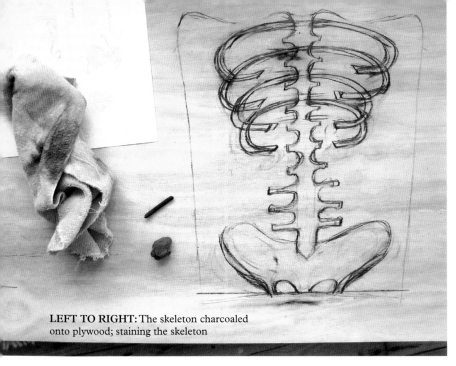

LEFT TO RIGHT: The skeleton charcoaled onto plywood; staining the skeleton

step 1

Choose a piece of solid wood the same thickness as the wood of the back rail and sides. Turn the wood so the grain is vertical; this will add much more support and structural integrity once you've cut pieces of spinal column no wider than an inch. Measure the height of the back of the chair so it will fit into the space allotted. In our case it was 15x20".

step 2

Draw the spinal column, sacrum, and pelvic bone onto the wood with a stick of charcoal, and keep in mind that even though the grain is vertically oriented, the chair will be no stronger than its smallest vertebra.

step 3

Draw the ribcage. We drew ours more stylized than an actual ribcage, more in keeping with the shape and balance of a Chippendale splat than an anatomy lesson. Wherever the ribs cross over one another you'll have to make the cuts separately, so keep that in mind as you curve the ribs.

step 4

Drill holes in any of the spaces between ribs, and anywhere there is a closed space. This hole will be where you'll insert the saw blade.

step 5

Illustrated here is a scroll saw. You could cut it with a handheld jigsaw as well, but a scroll saw is easier on your arm and more precise. Move the wood through the saw, but don't push it through, or else you run the risk of breaking the saw blade.

There is only so much room inside the saw for a piece of wood as large as the back, so be strategic, and cut away all the outside edges first, width edge facing the back of the saw. Save the odd-shaped scraps; if you have kids, you could make a very interesting Matisse-like block game. Or you could do this with a different board while you have the machine set up. There's no need to be as beautifully clever as an Enzo Mari animali puzzle, but just some nebulous amoebas would make a super-fun toy.

step 6

Once the skeleton is all cut out it needs to be sanded to match the side rails of the chair back, so it flows seamlessly with the look of the chair's craftsmanship.

step 7

The skeleton now needs to be pegged into the back. To do this, drill shallow ½" holes down into the top of the spine, the two top ribs, and three across the bottom pelvic bone. Twist in a 1"-long wooden dowel the same width as the holes. We used a ⅜"- drill

and peg. Line the skeleton up with the chair frame and mark where the pegs hit on the bottom and top rail. Drill similar holes in these spots, then carefully tap the frame onto the torso with a rubber mallet. You may want to smear some wood glue on the dowels for extra strength.

step 8

Stain the new wood to match the chair. Chippendales were usually made from mahogany, but you should compare your chair with a stain sample pamphlet from the hardware store, or bring it in to the hardware store and ask which would be an appropriately matching finish stain.

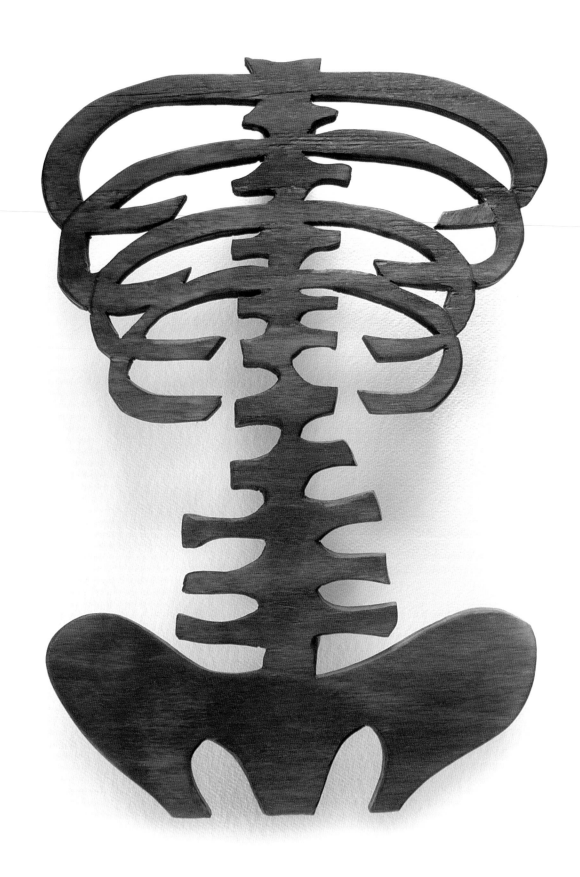

Hepplewhite

cut back
space like
monogrammed
Key

3 sided
Queen Anne

electric chair

This chair was in just about perfect condition for a certain aesthetic, meaning the patina was great, the wear was in the right spots, it was big and chunky and very Oxford-library looking. The only problem was that the leather on the seat had a huge worn rip extending from the back to the front. Likely this was because the stuffing had been matted down over the years and the leather was too stiff to handle all the up and down movement (keep in mind leather needs regular conditioning). On either side of the rip, the leather was dried out for a couple inches, so stitching it closed would require a fairly big patch, which would be none too subtle. The first thought that came to mind was Frankenstein because of the monstrous suturing involved, but it also had that very British Chesterfield back, which suggested Hogwarts. So fashioning a large Harry Potter–esque lightning bolt that would extend past the dried leather, we stitched together a chair suitably gothic for either Mary Shelley or J. K. Rowling.

step 1

Clean and condition the chair, until it is as pliable as possible. Cut a 30"-long pink metallic leather lightening bolt shape. Make sure the width covers the rip by at least 3" on each side.

step 2

We wanted the lightning bolt to have a border, to look more finished. This also added a third element and a third color, which balances out the design as a whole.

Cut strips of peach colored metallic leather, and machine sew them to the edges of the pink lightning bolt. Cut off any extra length to match the angles. Adhere this patch to the chair using E6000 clear glue.

step 3

With peach colored upholstery thread, thread a 6" curved-point leather needle and stitch the patch onto the chair. The glue will help it stay in place while you sew and also give it added strength. We let the tip of the lightning bolt hang loose at the bottom, since it looked better with the scale to have a longer bolt than one just covering the seat. We put a small stitch near the tip of it, to ensure it always was taut.

tools & supplies

- chair
- scissors
- pink metallic leather
- peach metallic leather
- sewing machine
- leather sewing machine
- needle
- E6000 clear glue
- matching upholstery thread
- 6" curved-point leather needle

pool noodle chair

I n the summertime you can't go to a yard sale without tripping over a polyethylene pool noodle (even if there's no pool). We'd never paid much attention to them until we found a bunch of dirty old foam insulation tubes on the street, which, much to Linda's dismay, were summarily tossed into the car. The plan was to make a chair with the tubes wrapped in patent leather, and somehow, maybe with a kind of hose clamp, worked onto a frame. The chair would look like a bowl, reminiscent of the Michelin Man, or Bibendum. Then we started noticing the pool noodles, which were much sturdier and cleaner than the insulating tubes, thus the better choice for the chair. But the dirty street tubes didn't go to waste as they were used for the prototype for the noodle chair, and will some day be made into an "antique" noodle chair. Prototype measured, we cut the pool noodles to size, but as we wrapped them with the patent leather, the resulting wrinkling due to the concave bend was too distracting from the shape. So we took off the leather and realized all that needed to be done was to simply gather the noodles together and curve them, letting the colors show. Plus, as there are no closed leather ends, with a slight shortening of the interior noodle, the 22 open ends could now act as insulating koozies for your favorite beverages. That's a whole case, if you have one in each hand.

RIGHT: Poolside in Old Orchard Beach, Maine

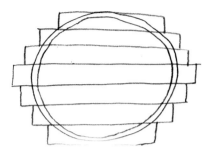

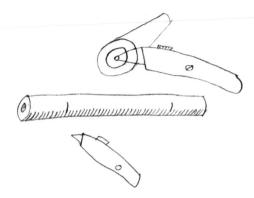

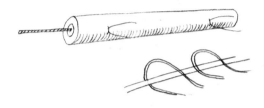

The pool noodles need a frame, but this is probably not something you can just go ahead and make, unless you're a welder or fabricator. We used the frame of an old round rattan and wicker chair that was falling apart. What you're looking for is any type of chair with a round ring frame, about the size of a hula hoop. In fact, you could use a hula hoop if you wanted yours to be a legless, floating noodle chair. Our chair was upholstered in wicker, so we sliced it off with a box cutter to reveal the rattan frame.

step 1

There are two sizes of noodles: the outside noodles are 3½" in diameter and have a 2½" interior, inside of which the smaller noodles fit. If you can't find these at a yard sale, try a hardware store in the summertime. The shorter end pieces can be made from one noodle. Fit the thinner noodles into the thicker noodles. Place one noodle across the middle of your frame, and bend it by pressing it into the back. Allow 5" overlap at either end of the frame. Mark for cutting.

step 2

If your center noodle measures 43" (which ours does) the adjacent noodles should be 1½" shorter, and the noodles adjacent to those, 1½" shorter still, and so on until the end pieces, which are about 3 inches shorter. By the way, if you did want to make this chair as a koozie holder then you should cut 4" off the ends of the interior noodles, to make room for a can. The easiest way to cut these is a retractable razor, pushed out to about 3½". You'll need a clean cut through the noodle or else it'll look a bit messy.

Once the noodles are cut, form them how they'll

tools & supplies

- ⅜" threaded rod
- hacksaw
- round framed chair
- nylon zip tie
- rubber coated wire
- plyers
- boxcutter

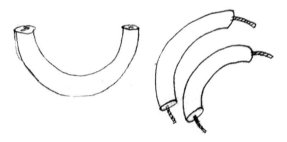

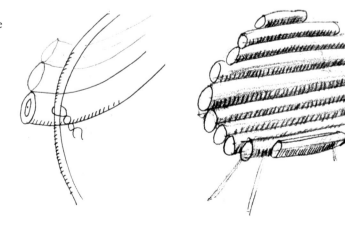

be onto the chair frame, and put a little mark at the point where the noodle meets the frame (the ring). Take the noodle away and cut a slice the width of the razor into your mark, halfway through the noodle. Now insert a loop of rubber-coated wire or a nylon zip-tie through each cut; leave the ends open as they will later be used to loop around the threaded rod. In the photos you'll see we used braided wire, but this was far too sharp. Actually I recommend nylon zip-ties, and later, after it's pulled taut to the frame, cut off loose ends extra close and turn the little lockbox end back into the noodle.

step 3

Measure out lengths of ⅜" threaded rod and cut these with a hacksaw, at lengths 4" shorter at each end than the noodles. These are the sturdy interior framework for the noodles, but you don't want them visible at the ends. Insert the rods into the noodles so the loop of wire or nylon tie you used is around the rod, and can be pulled to tighten.

step 4

With the threaded rod inserted, the noodles now need to be bent to fit in the chair frame. Make sure the zip-tie or wire ends face the frame. We found that bending them gradually across a knee works the best, and it's easy to control. Bend it a little, then fit it to the chair, if it needs more arch, then put it back over the knee; it's easier to bend forward than undo it backward.

step 5

Once a noodle is curved with the correct arch, attach it to the frame: place it on the frame, pull taut to the back, and twist the wire tight (or tighten the zip-tie). This is definitely easier with someone helping push the noodle to take up any slack. Start with the middle first. Next, push the next two adjacent noodles; they may overlap the central one a bit, but this is normal. Proceed, pushing the next higher and lower noodle simultaneously, until you reach the ends, which are by far the most difficult. If you use wire, make sure you twist it into a tight ball and tuck it inside itself so you don't inadvertently prick your hand.

TOP TO BOTTOM: the noodles in order; the chair in progress; wiring technique

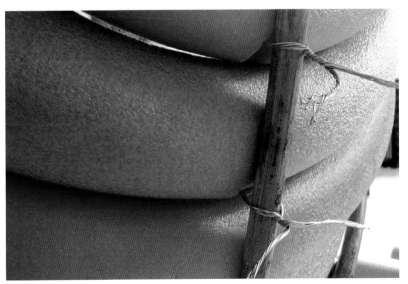

tables

There are so many materials available that would make good tables. Virtually anything with a flat surface can be put on just about anything else and you have a table. For instance, this book was written at a table made from two very old worn sawhorses with a sleek piece of glass on top. The sawhorses were from the sidewalk one fall and the glass was from a coffee table whose glass legs had broken. Most of the projects in the book were made on a 4'-square shallow plywood box screwed to an old table saw. We've included three tables that might inspire you: a simple marrying of a fairly common base with something not so common, a new use for an old basketball hoop, and a resourcefully utilitarian way of rescuing beautifully patinated old wood.

wooden slab table

This is a simple idea that we wanted to do for years, but never found a slice of tree in this proportion. We found our slab at a retired engineer's place in Maine. The tree slab was in perfect condition, with just hundreds of hand-saw marks striating wildly across the top. The little Eero Saarinen–style base originally supported a chrome diner stool, probably one of a dozen on a long raised platform in front of a counter. We fought the temptation to paint it white, instead enjoying the rare black paint and patina—although in this case I'm stretching the romantic ideal of patina. (The original pitted chrome seat was "patinated" enough for me to not even bring it in the car, and it was left at the yard sale.)

tools & supplies

- slice of tree
- chair base
- drill bit
- drill
- screws

The base has screw holes provided, but before you put in wood screws, take care to drill pilot holes so you don't split the wood. A pilot hole is a smaller hole drilled into the wood to ease the pressure of the larger screw being wedged in. Put the wood on the floor and drill the screws in from above.

ABOVE: A well-stacked pile of wood behind a yard sale.
RIGHT: the base at a garage sale

hoop table

This is a nice easy project. One day we came across this forlorn old basketball hoop. We measured the diameter, turned up the hooks a little with rag-covered pliers, and ordered a round top from the glass shop. Then we screwed the hoop plate into the wall. Try to screw into a stud behind the wall surface—these are the vertical 2x4"s that are the framework of the wall. Usually they're spaced 16 inches apart. The basketball hoop plate has holes 4" apart, so you'll only be able to fit one row into the 1½" stud. But even two screws into a stud is better than all four into plastic anchors, especially with something that is cantilevered.

Don't paint the hoop; just wipe it off with a rag and some Fantastik. Because you're only adding a piece of glass, there needs to be a strong balance between the two: a game of old vs. new.

tools & supplies

- basketball hoop
- glass top
- rag
- pliers
- glass
- anchors
- screws
- drill
- stud finder

picnic table

There's a type of table you come across at outdoor flea markets and county fairs that's made of perfectly grayed weathered wood. The design is strictly utilitarian, made of planks, square fence posts, and 2x4"s. Left out in the open year-round, the tables take on a beautiful silvery patina. Each time we saw them we were inspired, and always had a desire to build one of our own in the same manner. Luckily we live up the road from a working port and an old railyard, and between them there's a good chance that type of wood will materialize, whether it's from a thrashed wharf or a collapsed train car. Usually at industrial sites like these there is a surplus of materials that they're more than happy to have you take away. As it happened, one day a trailer appeared in the old pier parking lot piled with beautiful long boards of the perfect silver patina. We drove down, collected what we needed, and started designing our farm table. It shouldn't look exactly like a flea market table, but should still retain that utilitarian essence. So we thought, what would Jean Prouvé do (WWJPD)? The top would be like the floor of a Parisian apartment and the legs would be cubist rudders (TWJPWD).

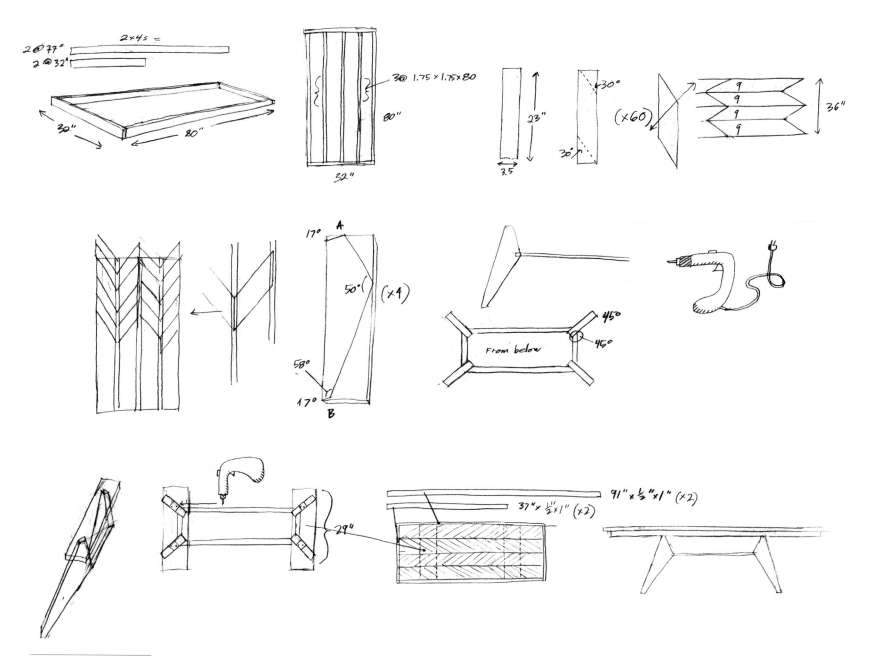

tools & supplies

- patinated wood planks
- 2x4"s
- table saw
- hand saw
- chop saw
- drill
- finishing nails
- hammer
- 2" wood screws
- 3" screws
- compass

step 1

Gather as much silvered, patinated wood as you can. Some of it, where weather has crept in a split, will inevitably fall apart, but by having surplus you should be okay.

Cut the four pieces of 2x4" that will be the frame for the chevron top: two side rails each at 77" long, and two end rails each at 32" long. Screw these together with the ends outside.

Inside that frame, evenly space three pieces at 1¾x1¾x80" each, and screw in flush with the bottom of the 30" side piece (flipped over, it should all be even).

step 2

The weathered planks measured about 8" across, so we ripped them down the middle and finished them to 3½"-wide lengths. These were then cut into 23" lengths. You'll need about 60 of these, so if you don't have an electric chop saw by now, borrow one. To cut these pieces into chevrons, angle the saw to 30°, cut each one at precisely the same corner point (clamp in a wooden guide), then turn them around and saw the other end to 30°. If your saw doesn't cut the angles all the way through, finish them by hand.

step 3

Starting with the middle rows, set the chevrons into place. The 6" angle should be along the center of the support rails. Evenly place the four rows of these down the length of the table. There is room for 11 complete chevrons on each row. Nail these into place with finishing nails. Dull the tips of the nails first by hammering them once on iron or stone—this allows the nail to "push" through rather than to pointedly "split" through. Place the end pieces on one at a time, and saw off evenly parallel to the end of the table.

step 4

For the Prouvé-style legs, we pulled 2"x8"x6' boards from an old floating dock. Cut four pieces of 2"x 8x28" board, then pencil on the lines of the angles provided in the sketch. At the leg's widest point it should measure 6½". Cut the legs.

step 5

The legs need to be connected together. We used four lengths of the same 2x4"s cut lengthwise (the same type that lays lengthwise and holds the chevrons). Cut the lengths to 43", including ends with a 45° angle; this will be screwed into the legs at the end of their widest point, as in the photos. Cut the width pieces to 21", also ending in 45° angles.

CLOCKWISE FROM TOP LEFT: profile of the table; The chevrons being arranged on the frame; sketching the legs onto a 2" x 8"

step 6

Cut two ¾" boards to 6x29". These will fit underneath the table and be screwed in from the sides, so double-check this 29" length to make sure it'll wedge in. Screw the two end legs together with the 45° cross piece, then screw the 6x29" board to the legs, drilling straight down into them from the top. Use a pilot hole so nothing splits.

step 7

Do the same to the other end, then connect the two end leg pieces together with the 43" lengths. Make sure everything is sturdy. Lay the top down, underside up, and fit the leg pieces into the frame, centered. The 6" board should be 11" from each end 2x4". Press down, and screw the board into the top with 2" wood screws. Drill pilot holes into the long side frame and screw 3" screws into the leg board from the sides.

step 8

Flip table over and measure the total width and length, which should be 36x90". Next cut edging trim for the top. We did this by ripping lengths of the edges of the 2"x8"x6' dock, at ½" wide each. Hammer these into the sides of the chevron top. Finis!

storage
74-103

storage

esides the chair, the most common piece of furniture that's kicked to the curb is the dresser. In most instances this is because of a simple malfunction: a knob fell off, a leg broke, a drawer stuck. Even if a side is all scratched up, or there are strips of veneer missing, it's still perfectly good as a simple fixer-upper, or as a raw material jumping-off point for a more elaborate project. Our "Le French Dresser" (page 78) was in a bit of a shambles when we salvaged it, but still, no need to send it to the landfill. Think about all that wasted energy: the space it takes up in a garbage truck and the gas it uses, all the resources it takes to burn an old dresser or make it into pulp and chemically treat it or all the energy used to make an entirely new replacement dresser. Before you put something out to pasture, or even before you go to the shop to buy a new one, think about at least a paint job, or half a paint job (page 98).

Along the same lines is the striped luggage project (page 82). If you think of each suitcase as a drawer, then a few of them become a dresser you could fit under the bed. Although hopefully once you customize them you'll want to show them off.

In some cases we've made storage projects that might be a little conceptual using the box/dresser theme; in other cases we've made a simple modification. We even used a canoe (page 86), which serves as a hold-all storage, but could with a little imagination and maybe a library ladder, be a pretty fancy "dresser." In both cases, the intent is to look at reuse and recycling from a design standpoint, to have you think "what if" and "why not."

le french dresser

Linda and I were in Maine gathering furniture and decoration for a friend's apartment in Brooklyn when we found this forlorn veneer dresser from the 1920s. We didn't need it for the apartment, but it had such nice lines and great proportions, that we knew in time it would likely come in handy. So we paid the $10 and threw the pieces in the car. It was slightly dilapidated but needed only minor repairs, of the tightening-screws variety. Soon it became the French Dresser resulting from our enthusiasm for typography and type designers, notably from the 60s and 70s, such as Milton Glaser, Herb Lubalin, and Lou Dorfsman. We're also fans of three-dimensional letters, which are of course everywhere, but when they're done well and kerned correctly they're always nice to see. In the mid-1960s Lubalin and Dorfsman joined legendary art directing forces to design and create a 40'-long wall of three-dimensional food words for the old CBS commissary; this was the main inspiration behind our dresser's facade. Originally we thought we'd just paint on the letters, since this was going to have to be done quickly as a last minute *Time Out New York* project, but decided if we were going to reference the CBS wall, then we should take no shortcuts. So we bought a scroll saw and some 2"-thick pine planks and were immediately excited to make a proper homage. The French swashy cursive text seemed a bit more stylish, the black and white paint referenced Chanel, and "les pulls" was a natural play on words, since the letters themselves were now going to act as the drawer pulls.

It's fairly simple to make, once you can get a handle on a scroll saw and realize it's not going to cut off your fingers. If you don't care to press your luck, make block letters using 1x2"s, which we're sure would look fantastic. We did include a 1x2" molding project (page 156); perhaps you can take some inspiration from that and make a custom molded-front dresser.

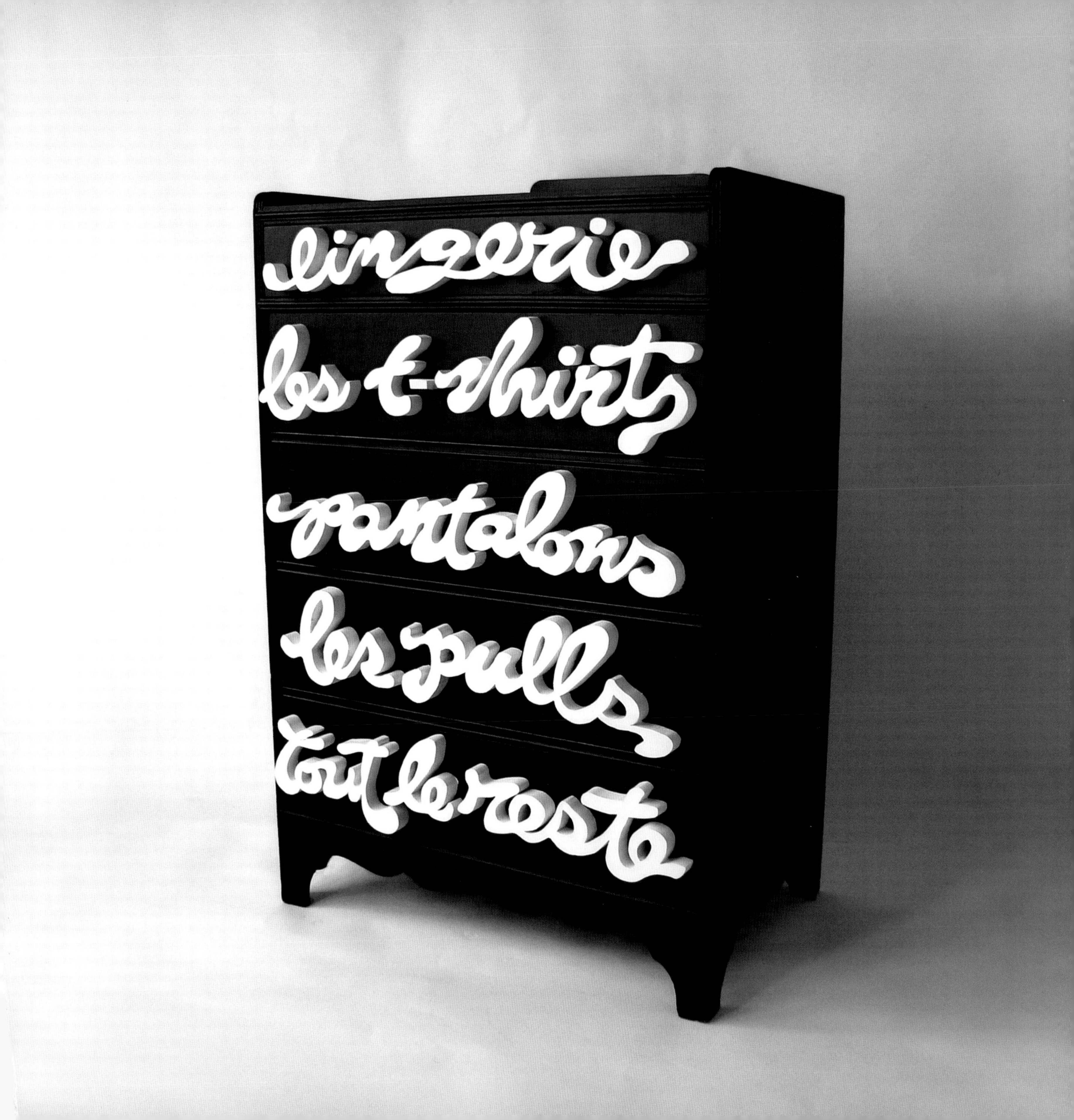
lingerie
les t-shirts
pantalons
les pulls
tout le reste

step 1

Our goal was to have the dresser painted a deep underwater black, with a slight residue of dark, dark green, like the inside of Davy Jones' locker. This is easy to do. First, unscrew the knobs and put them aside for a future project. Don't worry about the holes they leave, as you'll likely cover them with type. Sand the dresser with 120-grit sandpaper. This cleans the surface and will make the primer stick better. Next, apply the oil-based primer using a nice fine brush. Don't buy cheap brushes—you'll only get one use out of them and they'll leave annoying amounts of shed bristles in your paint job, some of which you'll find after the paint has dried. When the dresser is dry, go over it with 400-grit sandpaper.

step 2

Brush off any sanded primer dust with a damp rag. Prepare the paint in a plastic bucket, pouring in about 90% black and 10% green on top, not mixing them together—they'll mix as you brush the paint on the dresser. Start with the top and work your way down, brushing always downward. Paint the entire dresser, let it dry and paint it again. A second coat will protect the paint better and it's less likely to chip.

step 3

To make the words: measure the drawer fronts and mark this out on your planks of 2" pine. Write the words in cursive, and then trace around them to make them thicker. See opposite for a diagram of how we made each letter, from a line drawing to what it would look like in 3-D.

Once you have your type penciled on, drill holes inside all the letters with loops (e.g., e, p, l, s [sometimes], g, o, a). These holes will be where you'll drop down the saw blade to cut the precision loops. Next, fire up the scroll saw and start cutting. This sounds ominous, but you'll find that it's rather simple and far less nerve wracking than you might imagine.

If you're cutting a long word like "lingerie," you'll need to bisect it after the *g* so it fits into the elbow of the scroll saw. "Pantalons" was also too long, so we wrote it with a natural break after the *t*.

The scroll saw is like a sewing machine: there is a

tools & supplies

- sandpaper (120- and 400-grit)
- oil-based primer
- fine oil brush
- rag
- oil paint (black, dark green, and white)
- 2" pine board
- pencil
- drill
- scroll saw
- wood glue
- screws

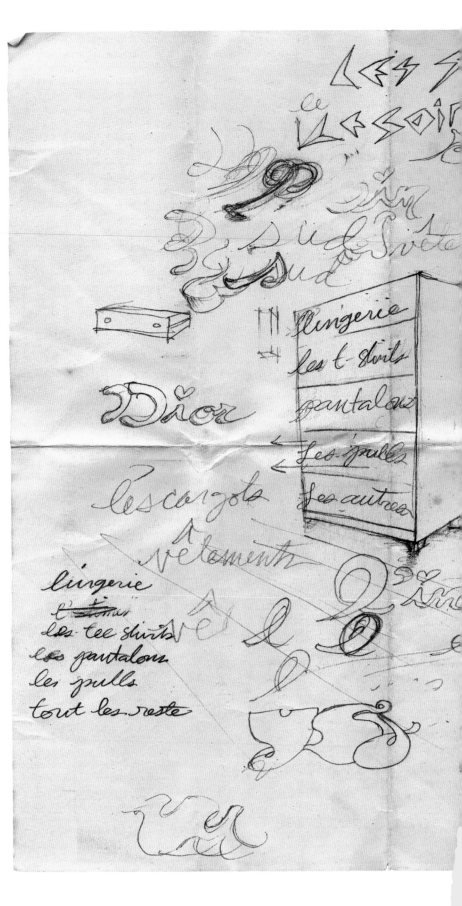

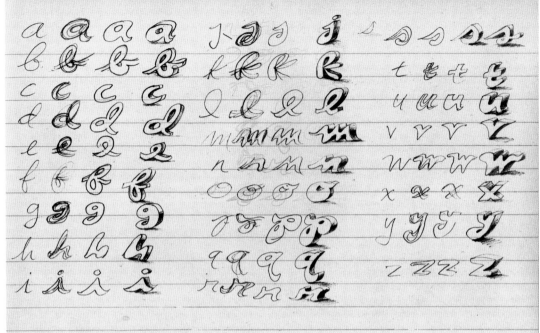

dial that controls the speed, and it becomes natural to constantly use it, especially in nooks, sharp angles, and small holes. One tip we've learned is to not push the wood through the saw too fast and forcefully or else you'll break the blade, which entails unplugging the cord, unscrewing the nuts that hold the blade, finding a new blade, trying to remember which direction the teeth go (down), etc. So remember, slow and steady wins the race.

step 4

Once you've finished the letters, sand them so there are no saw marks, dust them, prime them, and paint them. We used white, but of course you can use any color you like. After they're dry, glue them to the front of the drawers. After the wood glue is dried, screw the letters to the drawers from behind at the thickest loops. 1" screws should work, and drill a pilot hole first, but don't drill through a letter. Voilá!

striped luggage

In the glory days of travel people used to identify their luggage by having stripes painted on them. I'm not entirely sure what the significance was in regards to the colors chosen, but I'd venture to guess it could be heraldry colors, club colors, country colors, or if you had to paint your Louis Vuitton steamer trunk, one would think favorite colors. We did see a few suitcases at an auction up in Maine a couple of years ago from the estate of an expat Brazilian couple and the stripes were green and yellow. These days there's really no need to paint stripes on your luggage or suitcases other than just for the fun decoration of it. But, as we said about the wooden boxes, there is certainly always a plethora of vintage suitcases out there and you could easily put together a stylish suite with your own colors and initials. Or for that matter treat a wooden box like luggage and paint a stripe on that.

Of course you don't have to actually use the luggage. You could just pile it up along a wall and keep magazines in them, but we would still recommend painting at least a couple of them with stripes and initials, just for the stylish look. One thing though, however great looking old luggage is, it seldom escapes the bane of mildew. We've found that leaving them open in fresh air for a few days, or sometimes weeks, will put an end to any musty smells.

On the following pages you'll find instructions and some watercolored schematic ideas. Bon voyage!

tools & supplies

- luggage
- masking tape
- ruler
- white primer
- acrylic paints
- brushes
- examples of striping

step 1

If the luggage smells at all musty, leave it open out-of-doors for a few days or weeks. A screened-in porch or a carport is ideal. You can spray the inside with Febreeze to hasten the freshening.

When the luggage smells clean, you'll need to decide on a color scheme. Nothing is off limits here. On the opposite page are a few ideas, but anything goes: pink and purple is an always daring favorite, or green and red, blue and yellow, blue and gray . . . the possibilities are endless.

step 2

As well as standard stripes, feel free to make the stripe diagonal or in a lightning bolt. You'll need to wrap masking tape around the suitcase to make the borders of each color (see illustration). Use a ruler to mark where the edges will be. If your bag is really old and has a fragile material, test press and release the tape in an inconspicuous area. If your suitcase unpeels with the tape, you'll need to draw on the stripes freehand. Start by painting the primer. The reason for primer is that the color of the paint will be more vivid over white than over black or brown leather. Don't paint any trim; just stick to the body of the suitcase.

step 3

To paint a stripe right next to another one, the paint will have to be dry before you lay the tape down. Be careful painting at the tape's edge; brush either into the paint or use a flat-head stencil brush to dab on the paint. Initials are another option: these can be alone or combined with the stripes, but they're interesting also because they have a color scheme as well. Block letters are fine, and these can be achieved with the flat side of your ¼" or ½" brush and a steady hand. If you're up to it though, absolutely letter in Bodoni or Clarendon. Try Pistilli Roman letters plus the lightning bolt and you'll have the coolest luggage ever.

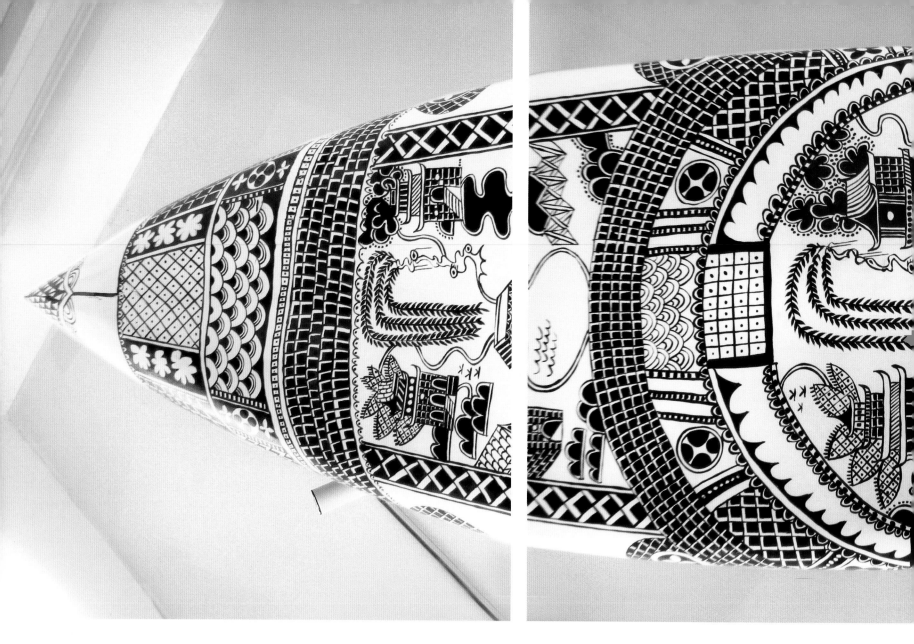

blue willow canoe

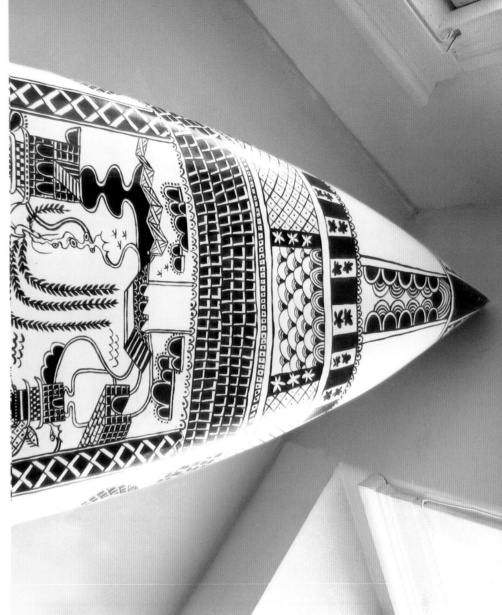

anoes abound in Maine, and this one was on the side of the road during a springtime bulky-item-pickup week. The owner was outside and he told us that he had a yard sale but no one was interested in a canoe with just a couple holes in the bottom, so sadly it was on its way to sink into the landfill before we rescued it.

We've always found the English Chinoiserie willow pattern intriguing in that there are so many variations, but fundamentally the graphic design has never swayed too far from the original 1780 engraving by Thomas Minton. In our case, we changed a few elements and modified some foliage with details inspired by English designer Celia Birtwell and Japanese Shinto symbols. On pages 28-29 you can see some conceptual sketches, which became so intricate we actually designed an entire dinnerware line called Pagodes des Arbres. The canoe, however, retained a more graphic approach, a little more primitive and folksy. For a third Blue Willow project, we found a tattered Herman Miller Eames chair and gave it the same treatment (page 24). Some day it could be installed in the canoe, and we'd have a vessel fit for an emperor. One of the thoughts we had while painting the canoe was, what if all the little blue and white pottery shards you find washed up on the beach, and in the soil came from big 18th-century ceramic canoes crashing and chipping against the rocks? Isn't that a possibility? So the project became a bit fantastical, but practically, we always knew that it would hang from the ceiling as a pretty fancy storage bin, storing polyfil and other lightweight items. Accessible by a stepladder, it could also be suspended by ropes through pulleys, so it could be hoisted up and down. And if we ever wanted to take it out on the water all we'd need to do is melt some silver into the holes, which is how the Chinese mended their own ceramics.

tools & supplies

- canoe
- latex primerpush pin
- string
- charcoal stick
- white latex paint
- blue enamel paint
- ½" oil brushes
- paper towels
- paint thinner
- two ⅜" hooks & eyes
- drill
- anchors
- rope or braided wire

step 1

We used high-gloss latex for the white, and navy blue enamel sign paint for the graphics. Any time you need to paint repetitive marks in the same color, oil-based paints are the best choice, since they glide in long lines from the brush and don't dry quickly like water-based paints do. Prime the canoe with any latex primer, then paint it with high gloss white latex paint. To make the circle in the middle and at the bow and stern, measure and stick a push pin into the middle of the bottom, tie a string to that, and tie a stick of charcoal to the other end (a 16' canoe would require an 8' piece of string). Start from the middle, drawing a light charcoal line up each side to the gunwale. Do this every foot or so, but remember there will be a large field where the pagodas are, with no lines needed.

Scaffold Knot

step 2

Decide where you want your fields of illustration to be, and with a ½" oil brush, paint the charcoal line borders. Don't bother wiping the charcoal off, as the enamel paint will absorb it.

The lines on our canoe averaged 1" apart. Obviously paint them as straight as you can, and if you make a mistake have paper towels and paint thinner handy. This will take off the enamel, but leave the white latex. Once you have two parallel lines, fill them in with squares, and fill those squares in with smaller squares in the corners. This pattern is called net-work, recalling the look of fishing nets. The best thing to have handy for a large-scale project like this is a layout you've done on a smaller scale, specifically in this case, a blue willow plate. You may decide you'd like the "petal" pattern on one border and the "fish roe" pattern on another, or the "Jooe Sceptre" mixed with "Y-work" and "trellis," or to have them all mixed up in one pagoda. It is a little intimidating being faced with having to choose what goes where on such a huge boat. If you find it difficult to paint freehand, then perhaps look into projection machines, which are available at many art supply stores, and then check out a book of blue and white pottery from the library.

To hang the canoe from the ceiling you may want to enlist the aid of a carpenter with some engineering skill, because the last thing you want is a boat falling on your head! If you insist on doing it yourself, use a stud finder to locate a ceiling joist, then drill a hole slightly smaller than the screw hook and eye you'll insert. The bow and stern should have a screw eye already; if not, attach one like the diagram. Suspend the canoe using any kind of nautical knot that appeals to you, or use braided wire.

CORWICO SPOOL WIRE
"FAVORITE" Assortment
48 SPOOLS
When You Want Spool Wire You Need CORWICO
CORNISH WIRE CO.,
NEW YORK

jewelry box

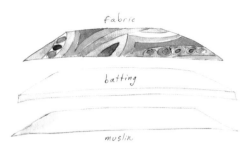

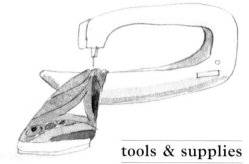

A perfect example of reusing something you already have, albeit not happily, this project came about due to Linda not wanting to part with a vintage Pucci blouse that our cat Waffles used as a climbing rope one day in the closet. Peppered with little holes and tiny rips up one side, it was now raw material. We were making the denim quilt at this time, and thought of using the same quilting idea, but in a small silk design; it might look pretty cool, especially with the thread naturally disappearing into Pucci's thin black line around each color. There wasn't enough fabric to make anything like a pillow or a throw, but there was a perfect amount for a jewelry box. We thought using an old box would balance nicely with the modern print. At a flea market in Maine we found the right size, which used to house spools, and even had "favorite assortment" printed on a label inside—perfect for a jewelry box. This is a great project for alternative quilting, in that you're just following lines and not tangling with all the little fabric scraps. Also think about quilting larger pieces than this if you want a throw or a bedspread, or imagine a great big Pucci headboard and matching duvet. Any fabric can be quilted like this.

On a wall in our guest bedroom there is a screen print of a sci-fi painting, and the spaceships, gamma rays, and planets are all stuffed with batting and stitched around their edges. We picked it up at a yard sale in Maine from a guy in a "you are here" (with arrow in photo of universe) t-shirt. He said his mother made it for him when he was young. I'd never seen anything like it and remember thinking how great it was that his mom translated this rather Raggedy Ann flat-doll craft into something as cool as a blown-up Isaac Asimov book cover. How this relates to our Pucci box is that it's the same concept of combining old with new, or modern and antique, country and outer space. It's not just putting Pucci fabric in an old box; it's quilting it before you put it inside, and doing that third thing that ties the other two together.

step 1

Measure the top of the box, then cut your top fabric to be 1½" bigger on each side. Do the same with the batting, and the backing fabric, which can be just muslin or a scrap of whatever's around—it's really just something to sew the top to and sandwich things together. Layer the backing on the bottom (good side down), batting in the middle, and chosen fabric on top (good side up). Choose a thread that either looks good and matches, or blends in completely. Use a quilting foot on your sewing machine if you can: this allows you to sew a few pieces of different fabric without them slipping around, which could result in frustratingly crooked lines. (Pins work well too.) Stitch all of the lines right off the edge of the fabric.

step 2

Measure the inside of the box, and cut a piece of scrap plywood to fit inside, minus ⅛"—this will give a little room for the quilted fabric to wedge down the side of the box and make a tight fit. Cut the board with a saw, and sand any rough edges so you don't have an accidental fabric pull. With the fabric face down, center the board and turn an edge of the fabric over the wood, and staple. Don't pull it too taut or it may pucker. Repeat this on the opposite side, then the two ends, stapling your way to the corners.

Turn the board over and fit it into the box. Fill with jewelry.

tools & supplies

- small box
- top fabric
- batting
- backing fabric
- matching or contrasting thread
- sewing machine
- quilting foot or pins
- plywood
- saw
- sandpaper
- staple gun

pipe umbrella stand

LEFT: The pipe at a construction site

tools & supplies

- steel pipe
- fence post chunk
- saw

We never really thought about an umbrella holder until we happened to come across this fantastic super-heavy steel construction pipe printed with a very smart Helvetica type. It was slightly too tall, so we inserted a chunk of fence post to raise the umbrellas to a proper height and to act as a rain run-off blotter. Odds are you may never come across this same type of pipe, but simple readily available white PVC pipe would achieve the same look, is easy to cut, and the thicker pieces have a nice weight to them. We would recommend screwing a few different thicknesses together, like the Sewer Pipe Lamp on page 116. You could also use a drainpipe for a play on the rain theme. Whatever you choose, have something in the bottom so you don't end up with water stains on your floors. On second thought, it might be interesting to have a floor with giant coffee cup ring marks on it, and giant crumbs next to it, like the remnants of a giant continental breakfast, without having to actually make the food (see Chaise-burger, page 40).

toy chest

We wanted to do this project for some time and finally came across the perfect box. The idea was to play upon scale, and also mix old with new, which is a recurring theme with us. In this case it was a Lego made relatively enormous and from wood. The box was dull pine, which was perfect for the primitive folk look we wanted (like a modern-day toy manufactured 200 years ago). The box didn't have a lid, so we inverted it, and luckily the bottom didn't have any feet or molding that would leave ghosts once they were knocked out of the way. Not that there's anything wrong with seeing the marks of the past, but in this case they might distract from the design; it's already got three things to take in: the wood, the scale, and the recognition that it's a Lego brick. The new bottom would be easy to make from scrap plywood, but finding the perfect size logs for the "posts" on top was likely going to be a tall order. A few months later we found what we were looking for along the waterfront when we came across some old pilings that were being replaced. The piling log was extremely dense and nearly impossible to cut with a hand saw. Our recommendation is to use a chop saw, table saw, or even a chain saw to section a log that's been underwater for some time. There's a definite difference between driftwood and wood that's been pegged into the seafloor for years. It also made the top ultra-heavy, but I suppose it'd make playing with toys all the more rewarding after hefting open what must seem like an iron lid. On the downside, your child might resignedly look at the lid with a sense of defeat and never put anything away. Alternatively, use tree branches or lighter materials.

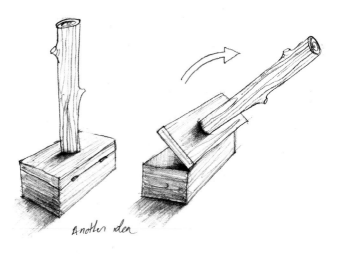

Another idea

tools & supplies

- large wooden box with no lid
- plywood
- power saw
- two 3" hinges
- thick branches, posts, or wooden poles
- wood glue
- drill
- six 2.5" screws

ABOVE: The lidless box at a yard sale.
BELOW: Scrap plywood heap by a railyard.

step 1

If the box has no lid, but the bottom looks great, you'll invert it and make a new bottom. You could do this in either of two ways: first is to make a bottom that fits inside the box, so you don't see it from the outside. Since the box is old it may not be square anymore, but if you trace the box on your plywood, you may have a difficult time cutting along warped lines. Instead, measure the sides—in our case they measure 22x40"—then measure how thick the box's wood is, double that, and subtract it from each side. This will make the box fit inside, and if it wasn't square before, it will be after you nail in this plywood. The second way to make the bottom is to skip the subtraction and just screw the new plywood into the sides, as pictured in the illustration (right). Either way is fine.

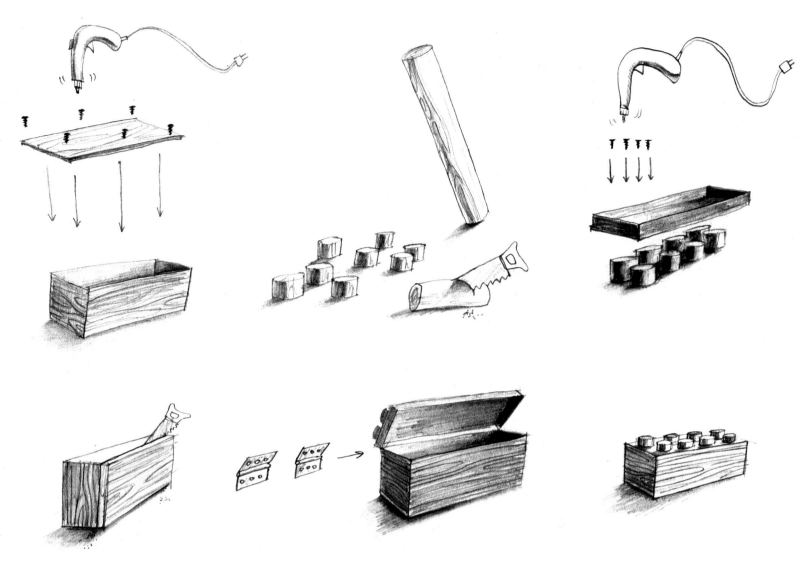

step 2

With a solid 6-sided box, now you need to cut the lid. Set the box on its side and measure 2" in from the aged top (which was the original bottom). Draw a line across each side at the 2" mark, and use a power saw to make a nice straight cut, lopping off the new top. As it's easier to hinge the top to the body while the posts are not yet screwed on, do just that. Then remove the screws from just the hinge's top half, and set the top aside for attaching the posts.

step 3

The posts on top need to be the right scale for the box, even a little exaggerated. One thing they shouldn't be is too small—it won't look right. Fence posts are a little heavy, so first look for a perfectly sized fallen tree branch. If you do use a fence post

or some piling, we recommend using a power saw to cut the sections. If you're feeling your oats, use a hand saw, but keep the blade perfectly square to the post and keep the post in a vise of some sort, or at least immovable, or else the saw will start swaying, and the worst thing you can do is correct for this, as you'll end up with a flat cone shape on the top of each post.

Once they're all cut in proportionate size, position them on the box top and secure them with wood glue. When it's dry, turn the lid over so the pegs are on the floor, and drill three pilot holes in each one. These are so nothing cracks or splits when you drill in the 2.5" screws. Once the screws are in you can now attach the top back to its hinges, and you're all done. Play well!

half painted dresser

We found this old 1930s dresser on an island in Maine. Our original plan was to paint the front and sides as you'd paint a wall mural, but the patina and aesthetic of the dresser proved too appealing to cover up completely, so we decided to paint just half. The dynamic Lichtenstein brushstroke served as a play on "painting" and contrasted perfectly with the antique side. It may look a little odd, but we're glad we did it like this. As nice as the Lichtenstein side is, it would have been a shame to cover the old black paint with its patina created by the cold salty air of a Maine island. So now it's like we have two dressers—a new one and an old one. It's perfect for one of those separated couples who have to live in the same house with a masking tape line down the middle. Unfortunately, the one who would have the Lichtenstein side would have no drawer pulls, as they were a little distracting.

We learned two lessons from this project: one was how to enlarge an image using a grid, and the other was to not rush into painting furniture. It's nice to have the right side of the dresser as a reminder of its history. Even though the patina was nice, I hadn't even really considered its provenance, and how it was really created. Sometimes these are more important values than if it's "clean."

Another lesson learned was not to be too enthusiastic with blue masking tape. If you're not going crazy with a power paint sprayer or a sopping roller, you can achieve a clean sharp line by just being careful. My mistake was pressing the tape into the dresser with such zeal that when the time came to peel it away, off came little bits of the prized patina.

LEFT: The dresser before.
BELOW: In progress

tools & supplies

- painters' tape
- oil primer
- oil paint
- oil brushes
- ruler
- charcoal stick

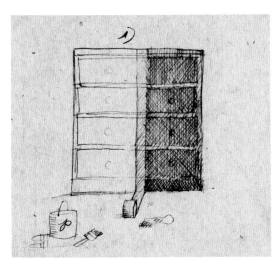

step 1

Mask the connecting edge of the side you don't want to paint with painters' tape. Make sure the edge, not the middle, of the tape is down the center of the dresser.

Prime with an oil-based primer. Let it dry and paint the background color if there is one (ours was white).

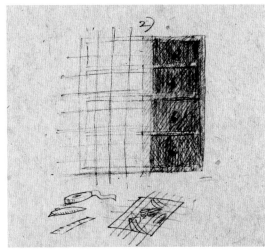

step 2

Select the image you want to paint, and using a ruler, dot the top and bottom edges of the paper, and both sides of the picture at every ½". Connect the dots to make a grid. Now do the same to the dresser, but make the grid larger (e.g., a 1"-wide grid would double your photo, 2" would quadruple it, etc.). Eyeballing may be the best course of action here.

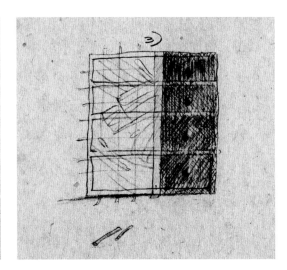

step 3

Transfer the image onto the dresser in charcoal, going square by square and correcting overall if necessary. With a graphic image like ours, you can be pretty accurate with the charcoal. Don't press too hard as sometimes charcoal is difficult to remove.

step 4

The Lichtenstein had only two colors, so like the order of a silkscreen process, we painted the red first. Paint the black lines last, as black covers up any other color. If you painted red over the black, for instance, you'd need more than a few coats to achieve a pure red.

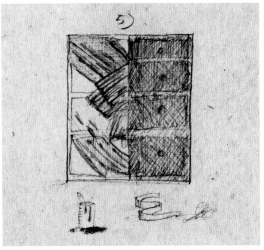

step 5

Last, carefully peel away the tape.

trunk seat

tools & supplies

• seat
• drill
• ¼" screws

Like an umbrella stand, an antique trunk was something we never thought we'd use around the house. Most seemed too hulking, too antique, and too *old*. In the summer of 2008 however *The New York Times* came up to Maine to write a story about yard saling with us. On a rainy day, with the panic of "we're not going to find anything" on our minds, we set out and at the first stop, grabbed this trunk just in case the rest of the weekend brought nothing but romance paperbacks and NASCAR debris (always a bummer). Fortunately that weekend turned out to be terrific, with virtually every garage sale presenting us with great stuff, including the shell of a giant Tahitian clam and Sam Haskins' *Haskins Posters*. Anyhow, the longer the trunk sat in the back of the car, the more we wondered why we never really looked at trunks before. It has great honey-patinated wood straps, perfectly worn orangey-brown leather straps, odd decorative touches, and a hand-rendered Futura typeface. Surely this would look pretty nice with some 70s stickers on it, showing it's not such a precious antique that it can't have some marks of

life. Or the handle could be replaced with a Massimo Vignelli–style rounded plastic rod pull or a bunch of blue and green ones, so it looks like the Pompidou Center. It had possibilities. What we did with it was conjoin it with one of its contemporaries—the back seat of a carriage. The result is extra seating and a perfect place to hide the recyclables bin. Mixed with a jade plant and a Cheshire cat, it's a scene right out of 1880 (which means it's time to balance it out with a Bertoia chair).

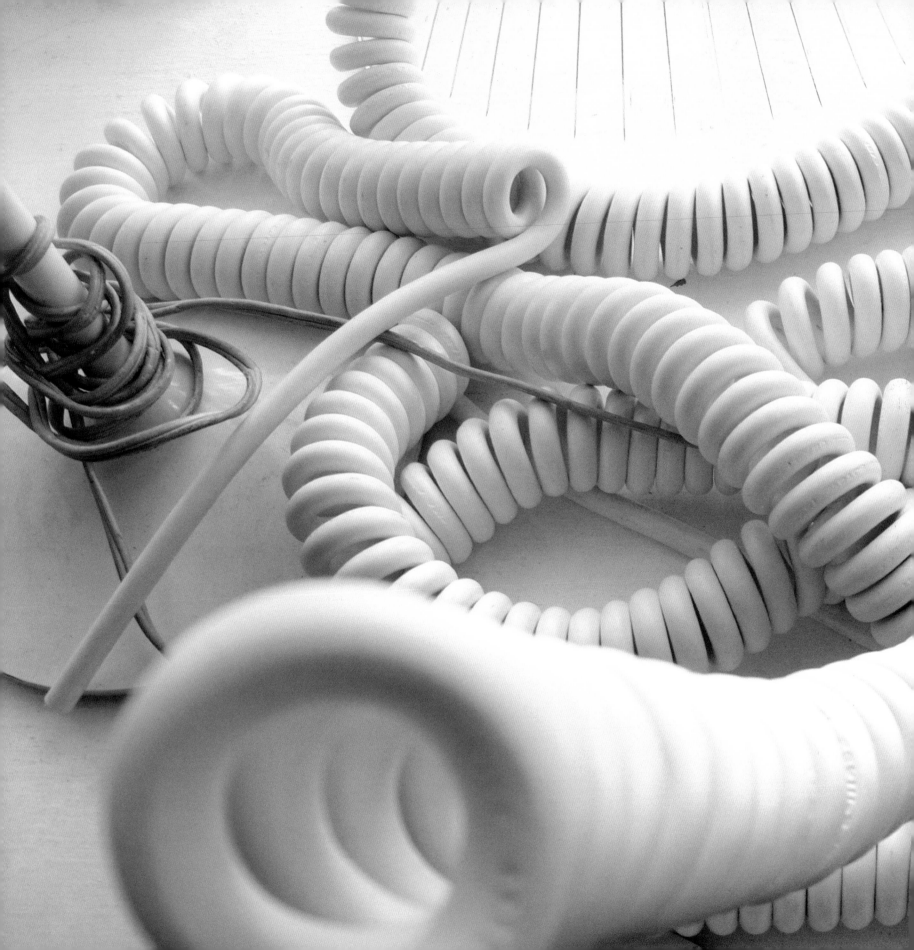

lighting
104-139

lighting

Lighting and lamps can be made from virtually anything. Any container can be a lampshade and anything else can be a lamp base. The object is to combine the top and the bottom into an attractive, cohesive, and balanced whole.

All of the items (or ideas) we used were found either at yard sales or on the side of the road. Obviously you can find perfectly good lamps at yard sales and if you're lucky on the side of the road, but we wanted to give you some ideas for what to do if you only found a part, or only had a notion.

The old pharmacy Funnel Lamp (page 112) is a case of how to make something if you've only found a pendant shade (or concave, open-ended). The Pastry Bag Light (page 120) is along those same lines, but with the cord considered. The Lightbox (page 108) is something you should know how to build, since its applications are legion. The Planter Light (page 134) is an exercise in enclosing a shade, the Sewer Pipe Lamp (page 116) is about structure, pigtailing, and the Beaubourg. In essence, the Football Task Lamp (page 126) and Turquoise Lamp (page 130) have to do with missing parts. But they all have to do with different ways of looking at things.

In a few cases we suggested a type of bulb, but in all the cases we made everything attached onto dimmer switches, which are either already on the wall affecting the outlet, or are plugged into a "line dimmer" available at any hardware store. A dimmer is a nice thing to have on any lamp, as it can turn bright lighting into "mood" lighting, flattering most everything around it as it also saves energy.

We've also included a simple spread on Basic Wiring (page 138), and once you master it you'll have so many ideas the light bulb over your head will be permanently aglow.

lightbox

One of the most fun and gratifying projects involving electricity is making a lightbox. Basically enclosed lamps, lightboxes usually have one illuminated side, made of Plexiglas or frosted glass, although there could be two sides, three sides, or even all six sides, in which case it would be literally a box of light. Of course the "box" doesn't need to be six sided either; it could be L-shaped, or L-shaped with another perpendicular leg, or five more, or 50 more—the possibilities are endless. The 90° angle box is the starting point for any sort of combination, so that's what we made here. It's also not necessary to have an entire side lighted. In the photo opposite, imagine the lighted side half covered with a board, or three small boards, or an entire plank with a knothole in it (this then becomes a lighted dot). If you took the plank off and used a jigsaw or scroll saw on it, then you'd have a sign. You could take Le French Dresser (page 78) and instead of using the positive letters, use the negative space left behind to become the front of your light box, making it Le French Shelf. Or change the scale and make it very wide and very long, with the Plexiglas and cutout at one end, making Le French Platform Bed. Or imagine the box opposite in your door frame, or on either side of a mirror, or as a mantle (page 196), or out in the yard as a Donald-Judd-meets-Dan-Flavin sculpture. One you learn how to make this—and it's simple—you'll always think of reasons to make more.

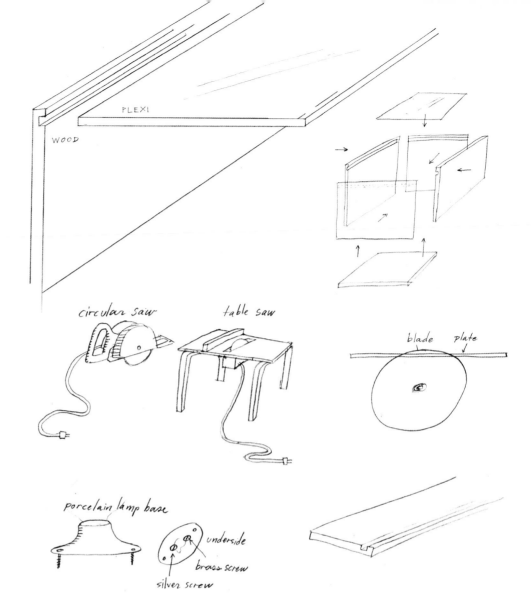

tools & supplies

- wooden box or wood
- ⅛" translucent Plexiglas
- table saw
- blade for wood
- blade for plastic
- mask and goggles
- white paint or Contact paper
  (optional)
- electrical cord
- socket
- plug
- lightbulb
- drill
- screws or nails

step 1

Basically, if you know how to wire a socket then you know how to make a lightbox. The simplest way to make the box part is not to make the box at all, but rather take an existing one and put a Plexiglas front on it. That's what we did here; our box started out as the note "D" of a demolished church's dilapidated pipe organ. Choose a box that's tightly made, as you don't want any odd light leaks. If you want to build your own that's even better.

step 2

To make a box, refer to Art Base (page 144). The only difference is cutting the grooves into the interior walls of the box to hold the Plexiglas. In order to do this you need a table saw. In woodworking-speak, the grooves are called dados, and there is a saw blade that cuts a dado, but they're also made by making two passes with the wood, with the fence moved slightly outward.

Gather the boards together and figure out where you want the Plexiglas light panel to be—in this case at the front, about ¼" away from the edge. Set the table saw's fence ½" away from the blade and ¼" above the plane of the table itself. Best thing to do here is refer to the owner's manual under "dado cuts."

step 3

Once you have the dados cut, you need to cut the Plexiglas, which can also be done on the table saw, but with a thinner blade that has more teeth for finer cuts. Always wear a mask and eye protection when sawing, especially with Plexiglas—breathing in plastic dust is awful. Cut the Plexiglas so it is ½" bigger than the box's interior (the dado groove should be ¼" all around). Before you put the saw away, fit the box together without screwing it closed, to make sure everything fits and no more cutting is necessary.

step 4

Because our box was so long, we needed many
bulbs pigtailed together. You may want to line the
inside of the box with either white paint or Contact
paper (as we did here), to ensure the light is bright
and even, with no hot spots. Keep the bulbs away
from the Plexiglas; in our case since we didn't custom make the box, the bulbs needed to lean a little.
If they were right up close to the plastic we'd have
had hot spots, maybe causing the Plexiglas to melt
(a possible fire hazard). We recommend CFL or
low-wattage bulbs as well—you don't want it getting
too hot inside. Using a porcelain lamp socket that
screws into the wood is a good idea since it keeps
the bulb in one place.

step 5

Drill a hole in the box where you want the cord to
come out and then assemble the pieces. You could
either nail or screw the box together, but stay away
from wood glue, since when the bulb burns out
you'll need to open the box in order to change it.
Try experimenting with different power switches.
Pictured here is a vintage one we found at a yard
sale which unfortunately never actually worked.

funnel
lamp

At a yard sale one weekend there was a
beautiful old, thick glass cone on a table
of odds and ends, the kind of object you'd
see at a posh antiques shop. At first we
thought, "That'd be a great lampshade
for *Tossed & Found*," but resigned ourselves to the
thought that it was likely too perfect to be anywhere
near affordable, not unlike the cliché too-pretty girl
who you'd never looked at twice, but then you end
up going to the prom together. The sticker read "$5
old pharmacy funnel." So in that regard, it was nice
that first off it was really great looking, and second
it was surprisingly cheap. Always keep in mind if
someone has a yard sale, they might as well just be
bringing stuff out to the curb—they don't want it
coming back inside.

ABOVE: The funnel at its yard sale

Our funnel has great hand-blown ridges inside, probably as a means for things to pour down more easily. In this case, the ridges refract the light, sparing your eyes from looking directly at a bare bulb. You need to use a clear bulb with this shade, to bring out the "sparkling" qualities of the glass. Always match the bulb to the shade: if the shade is meant to sparkle, like a chandelier or tinsel on a Christmas tree, use clear bulbs. If it's anything else, use a frosted bulb. For example, the Lightbox (page 108) needed an even, frosted light—if we'd used clear bulbs there would have been little "hot spots."

Put the cord through the funnel and tie a knot in it, leaving enough cord for the socket to hang in the middle of the shade. Follow the basic wiring guide (page 138) to attach the socket. Because the glass is so heavy you may need to suspend the weight of it by a wire. In this case, you can knot a wire around the knot in the cord, or just make a big knot in the wire that's for sure not going to slide out the top of the funnel, and suspend it by that.

We used a reproduction Edison bulb inside, which is an old clear glass bulb notable for a rather loopy filament.

tools & supplies

- funnel
- electrical cord
- socket
- lightbulb
- plug
- picture wire

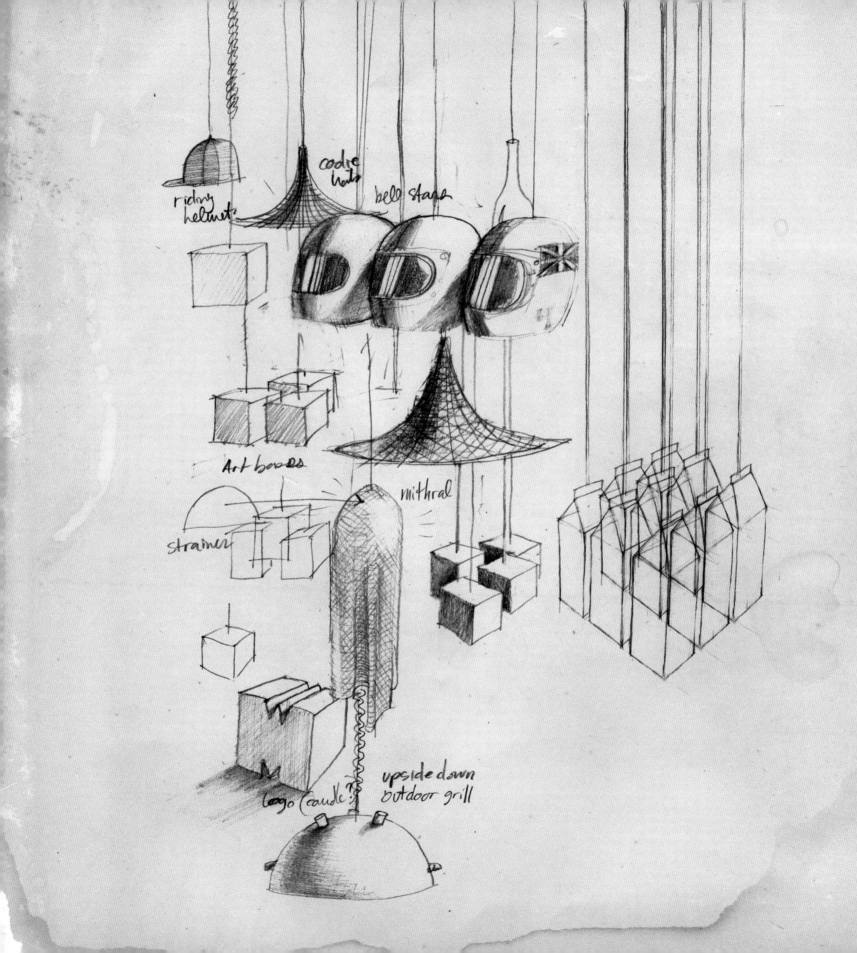

riding
helmet

codie
hats

bell stand

Art books

strainer

mithral

logo candle?

upside down
outdoor grill

sewer pipe lamp

Otherwise known as SDR35, this polyvinyl chloride (PVC) tubing is a pretty common material to find at any construction site, where it's cut into different sizes for drainage. It also comes in different widths, from as small as 4" to as large as something you could walk through. Before they bury it, it is cut to fit whatever schematic is underground. This means that there are plenty of off-cuts lying around.

There was a movement in late 60s/early 70s in Italy where domestic design was seemingly made all out of plastic, and all very stylishly. The Italians were making the coolest designs in the world: plastics were rounded, minimal, and groovy, and made into everything from furniture to dishes. Our idea for this drainage pipe lamp was inspired by the wildly simple designs of those Italians.

We designed it to look somewhat like a tree, standing on its trunk and branching off into other limbs. Each branch has its own lightbulb. This is relatively easy to do, as it's just a matter of pigtailing the wire together.

There are countless different formations you could make with this simple tube. Combine wide ones with narrow ones, cut them on angles, cap them with elbow flanges, suspend them, or use different colors. Green is for septic drainage, but the pipe also comes in white, gray, and blue, as these serve different functions, like the pipes of the Pompidou Center, come to think of it. Why not combine all the colors and make your own Beaubourg lamp. Ah, *l'esprit d'escalier*!

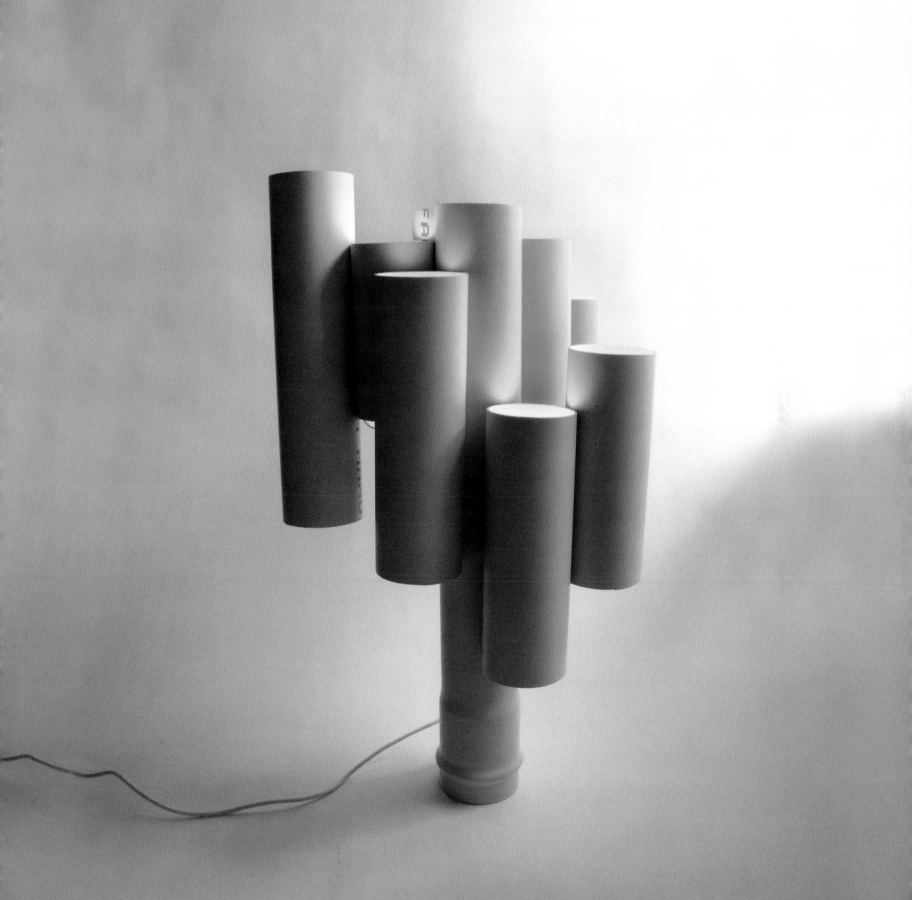

tools & supplies

- PVC pipes (about nine 14")
- PVC saw
- Drill with ⅜" bit
- ⅜" wing nuts, bolts
- candelabra sockets
- candelabra bulbs
- electrical cord and plug
- plastic epoxy

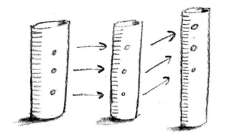

step 1

With a PVC saw, cut the pipe into slightly different lengths. Have one section that will be the "trunk," and use the wide flange end of the pipe as the base, for more stability, or if you have different widths, use the widest. You could even put this on three legs, or four, as a take on the aerial roots of a Banyan tree.

step 2

Have about nine pieces, approximately 14" each. Starting with the middle pipe, drill three ⅜" holes in the side, about 4" apart. These need to be vertically aligned with one another.

step 3

Drill the exact same hole in the adjoining piece. The middle hole is for the cord; the upper and lower holes are for ⅜" bolt and wing nut. Drill holes in each pipe.

OPPOSITE: The pipe
at a construction site
ABOVE: Conceptual
sketches of PVC pipe

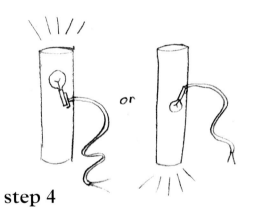

step 4

For the electrical wiring, use candelabra sockets—
these are thinner than regular sockets and better
for the smallish diameter of the pipes. You'll need
to make nine wired sockets, and they each pigtail to
one another, and to the middle (see Basic Wiring,
page 138).

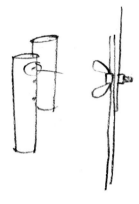

step 5

The inside of the tubes are too small in which to
turn a wrench. To hold the sockets in place, which is
tricky, you could use a few methods. You could cut a
round wood disc the same diameter as the pipe interior to act as a support or fashion a springy metal
clamp. But the easiest way is to use a fast-drying epoxy—the kind that comes in a syringe. Epoxy these
only after all the wiring is put together and tested.
Make sure the lightbulbs don't extend past the top.
Using wing nuts is easy since you turn them with
your fingers. Also they are a good foundation for the
epoxy to hold the sockets.

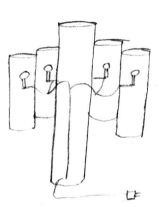

step 6

Drill a hole at the bottom of the middle base. This is
where the main pigtailed cord comes out and ends
in a plug.

pastry bag light

Years ago, designing the store-opening displays for an Anthropologie store, I'd used a bowl of stuffed pastry bags, with fountains of white coaxial cable spewing out of them Murakami-like into the air spelling, "If I knew you were coming," in reference to the 1950 Eileen Barton song, "I'd've baked a cake." The bags didn't light up, but I thought it would great if they did, and this was a chandelier, and not just a big "sculpture."

Years later Linda and I were at a yard sale where there was a bag of old cake-decorating equipment, and I thought the time was right to revisit that chandelier in a cleaner, more linear way. We took away the lyrics, and thought instead about a take on decorative ceiling plates, which traditionally go above a chandelier, to hide the electrical work. The pastry bags would shoot out streams of round electrical "icing" cord, ending in coils of cones and squiggles like an imaginary covered cake, or an extravagantly whimsical ceiling plate.

The pastry bags are made of plastic-lined linen; they give out a very nice glow from candelabra bulbs, and they're fairly calm looking, so it's a nice contrast when you do notice the "icing" on the ceiling. It's also nice to use the electrical cord as an object and element in its own right.

Another idea would be to use oil cans as the shades, with lines of shiny round cord up to either a crazy pile up or just a big black stain, like a pen that's leaked through a shirt pocket.

ABOVE: The vintage cake decorating items from a yard sale.

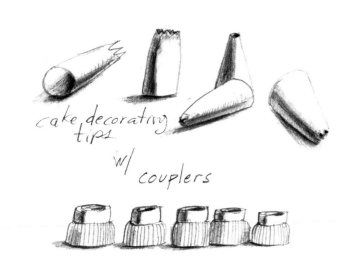

cake decorating tips w/ couplers

candleabra sockets   candleabra bulbs

tools & supplies

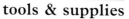

- white rope or cording
- white drillable bowl, about 18"
- drill with bit same size as lamp cord
- glue gun
- cake decorating tips
- pastry bags
- bag couplers
- 1" corner braces
- candelabra sockets
- candelabra 25-watt frosted lightbulbs
- electrical round cord
- wire nuts
- plug
- anchors
- screws

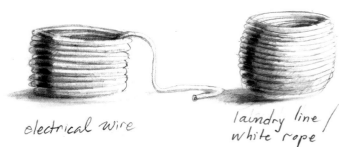

electrical wire   laundry line / white rope

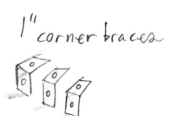

1" corner braces

glue gun

ABOVE: The coils in progress

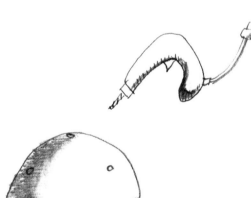

step 1

First, make the coils. A coil is meant to look like a pile-up of frosting from a long-pouring pastry bag. Originally we made these using the actual electrical cord, and it looked good and held for a while with just hot glue, but now our suggestion is to use either a laundry line–style white rope, or cotton cording from a fabric store. These will hold a tight coil better. Ideally, this whole decorative ceiling piece would be made from either injection-molded PVC, or ceramic like a coil pot gone awry.

step 2

Once you have five coils made, position the coils on your bowl or "base" as we'll call it. Drill holes in the base, the same diameter as the lamp cord. This should be a tight fit, since you'll be pulling the cords down to bring the bags into position. So if your lamp cord is ⅝", use a ⅝" drill bit. If you drill the holes too big, or the cord is loose somehow, clamp the cord with binder clips on the inside of the base. Drill another hole at the rim of the base, this is where the cord to the outlet will go through.

step 3

Cut five long lengths of electrical cord, put each one through a coil, then through a coil in the base. Using a hot glue gun on the (flared) edge of the coils, affix them to the base with the drilled hole in the middle. When they're all on, you'll have blank space around them. This is where you glue other spirals and hoops and squiggles of cording to disguise the base and make it look like a giant heap of frosting. Try not to make it a giant heap of hot glue. If you do, wait for it to dry and pluck off the web-like strands and little clear dots.

step 4

On the "bag end" of the electrical cord, before you put the candelabra sockets on the ends, unscrew a tip coupler; there is half that goes inside the bag first. Now slip a cake decorating tip, the tip coupler, and the pastry bag with the other coupler half over the cord. The tips come in all shapes and designs, so be creative. On the cord, screw the coupler halves together. Now move the bag up the cord out of the way and assemble the candelabra sockets, followed by 25-watt *narrow* frosted light bulbs (you don't want them touching the bags).

step 5

Up at the other end, the electrical coils that went through the base now need to be pigtailed together, and then pigtailed to a long cord that will go to the outlet, through the hole you already drilled. There's a pigtailing diagram to the right, and also on Basic Wiring (page 138).

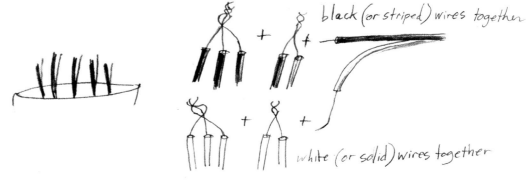

step 6

Attach four 1" corner braces to the rim of the base (see right). One leg of the brace needs to be inside, bolted to the base, and the other leg either inside or outside the base. Outside is easier to attach to the ceiling. If you choose the inside system, you'll need to screw those braces into the ceiling first, then slip the base over and bolt it in. With all the cords and bags attached this gets pretty heavy and unruly, so we suggest the outside method. Hold the base up to the ceiling and pencil a mark where the brace hole is, drill a hole in the ceiling for an anchor, then hold the base up again and screw the braces into the anchors. Disguise the cord with the plug end on it against a wall, or down some molding. You can pull the pastry bags down evenly (as shown), or in a spiral cascading design, or just randomly. Plug into a line dimmer. Do not lick the bowl.

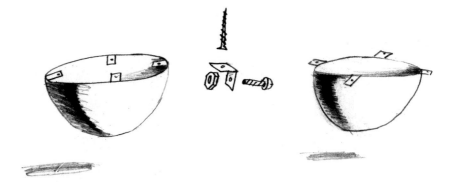

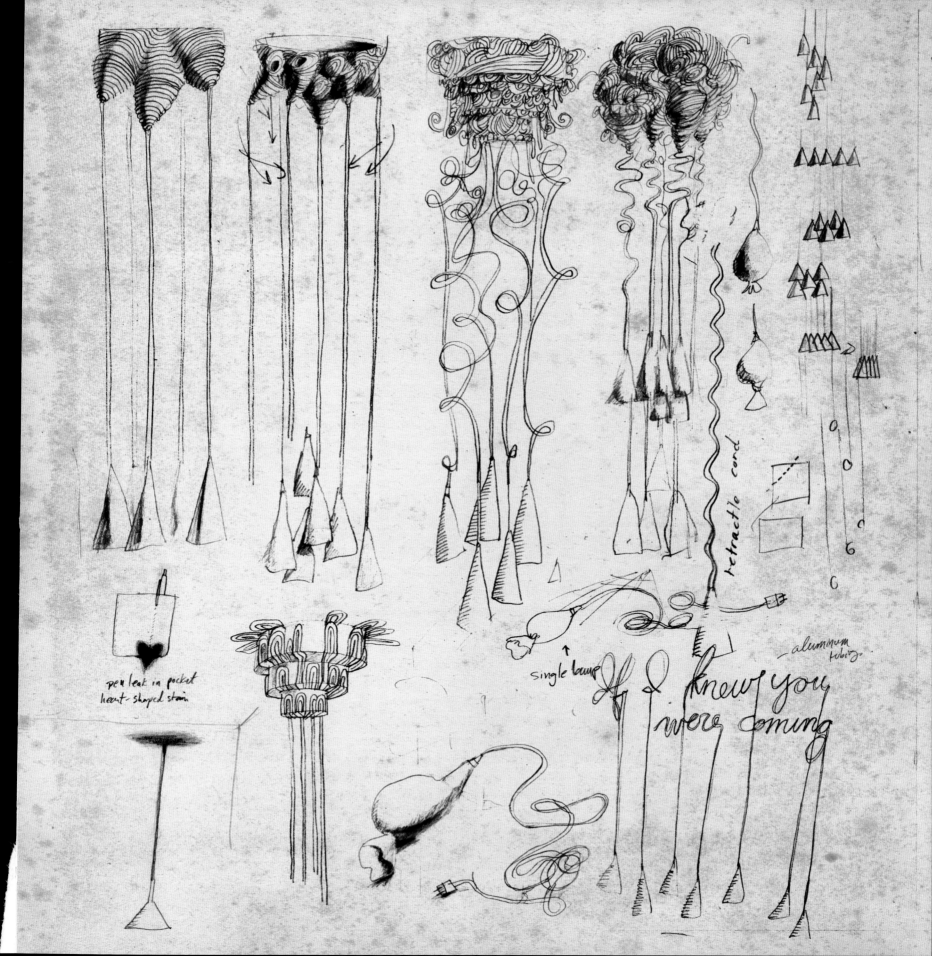

pen leak in pocket
heart-shaped stain

retractile cord

single lamp

aluminum tubing

If I knew you were coming

football task lamp

Somewhere along the line we started collecting task lamps. Sometimes called architects lamps or drafting lamps, they're a fairly common find at yard sales and flea markets. At one time our goal was to have a desk with a dozen white ones lined up on the front. That accomplished, it became a bit distracting sitting at the desk and being overwhelmed by that many lamps—somewhat like a *War of the Worlds* diorama. We took them down, but having so many gave us the freedom to experiment. The leather idea sprung from the rubber blades of an old Italian desk fan we had (the balance of nature and technology, allowing rubber is nature). To make a leather task lamp shade would be somewhat difficult, involving a cage and a leather sewing machine, but luckily a football was the perfect shape, and luckier still we happened to find one at a flea market with the perfect look of wear and age—a nice contrast to the white metal of the lamp. The leather lamp shade in general is a neat idea, and this half-football could be suspended as well. Also nice would be other old sports balls—medicine balls, rugby balls, tether balls; a suspended soccer ball would look great, all old-white and halved on the thick leather hexagonal seam, like a Buckminster Fuller dome.

tools & supplies

- chalk
- football
- scissors
- task lamp
- nuts and bolts (optional)
- drill
- ⅛" drill bit
- ¼" drill bit
- screwdriver

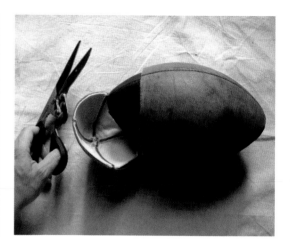

step 1

Mark a chalk line around the football, 1" in front of the stitches. There is a leather placket inside, and by cutting an inch past the stitches you'll clear it. If you cut through the stitches, they'll unravel.

step 2

Slit the leather. Inside the football there's a cotton lining that is stitched to the four seams, so cut right through this. Don't however, cut through the rubber bladder, as this is somewhat interesting and you might want it later, even to toss around. Cut all the way round, and pull the bladder out of the valve hole.

step 3

On the task lamp, you want everything but the metal shade. Depending on the brand of lamp, this may involve a hacksaw, or it might just be a matter of undoing a couple of screws. The goal is to get to the point where you have two, three, or four screws on some plate that can be screwed into the ball, like in the photo opposite. You may need to get new nuts and bolts, if the lamp was just riveted.

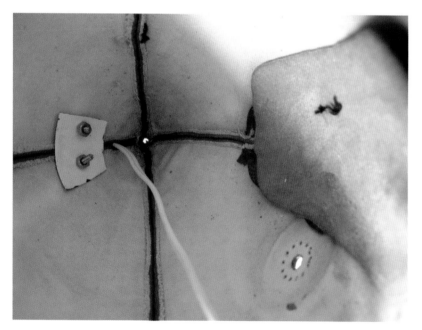

step 5

Undo the electrical socket from its wire. Poke the wire through the football at the hole between the point and the screws. Pull in some slack and reattach the socket. If you forgot how, refer to Basic Wiring (page 138). This socket now gets pushed through the hole at the point. It is held in place by a washer and gasket that is part of the switch—they sort of tighten the leather between them.

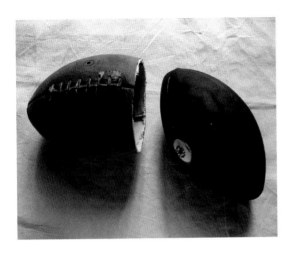

step 4

Use a ⅛" drill bit to drill screw holes into the leather. Fix the top of the lamp to the football at a balanced spot— the closer to the middle the better; we used the existing part of the lamp where the screws were in the first place as a reinforcing plate inside the ball (see photo). A piece of sheet metal would also work. Above that, drill a hole for the cord, and at the very point of the ball drill a ¼" hole for the lamp switch.

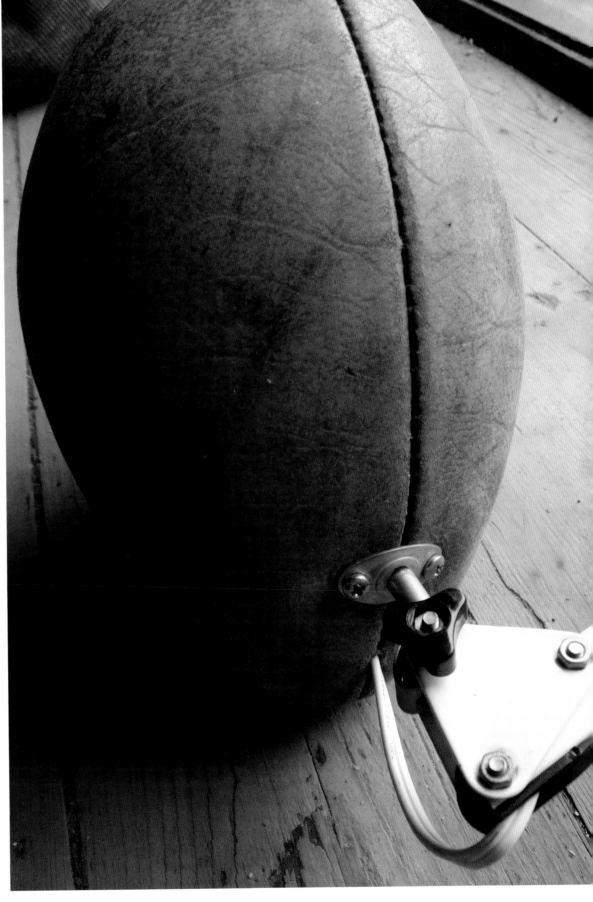

RIGHT: The task lamp connected to the football.

turquoise lamp

Chunks of Styrofoam flotsam are a fairly common sight in any seaside town. They are used to float docks, piers, wharfs, and rafts, but are not the hardiest and tend to fall apart and float away after a few bad storms. Luckily by that point they've already attained a nice maritime patina of crags, algae, rust, and if you're lucky, barnacles. The one we've made into a lamp reminded us of a giant piece of turquoise and we thought it would look fantastic in a Southwestern American Indian–themed home, and for that matter in a Northeastern home, where it would be recognized as a piece of dock, albeit cleverly made into a lamp. Another piece of flotsam that's easily beach-combed are burned logs. These are just pieces of

driftwood that have been used in a bonfire, but you could imagine them being the unfortunate mast of some long-ago shipwrecked schooner, and no doubt they would look super cool as lamp bases, and witty, especially that they're burned. Last summer we found a burned log that we could have sworn was an old pirate's wooden leg (slightly gruesome); we liked the turquoise better. However, if you do make a lamp from a log, you'll need to buy an extra-long drill bit, because the duct tape directions (next page) won't work.

This project is also an exercise in basic table lamp-making, and you can see that with a little imagination and just basic electrical know-how, virtually anything can be made into a lamp.

sand filled

1/4" wires

tools & supplies

- flotsam (Styrofoam or driftwood)
- ⅜" threaded rod
- duct tape
- drill
- ⅜" drill bit
- lamp kit with harp
- lamp shade

step 1

You'll need to make a plumb hole down the middle of the Styrofoam. This is for the length of hollow threaded rod that houses the lamp cord and screws into the bottom of the socket. At the hardware store, make sure you get the right width threaded rod for the socket. You can make the hole using the threaded rod: since Styrofoam is so soft, you can duct tape a drill bit to the end of the rod, the tighten the other end to the drill. Or you can buy a long drill bit.

step 2

Once the hole is drilled, attach the wiring. Put the lamp cord through the rod first, then through the Styrofoam, so you don't have to take it all apart later if you forget. If you find that the cord gets in the way of the Styrofoam sitting on a table evenly, either cut away a groove for the cord, or put little adhesive pads on the bottom. Use a socket with a harp, so you can put a shade on the lamp. The shade we used was from a yard sale, and had an appropriate matching patina.

planter lights

These hanging pendant lamps were something we came up with while on a trip to Buffalo. After a dark and stormy night, we went yard saling and noticed, amidst fallen tree limbs and power lines in the middle of the road, a pair of marble urns knocked over, yet kind of swaying around in the breeze. On closer inspection they weren't marble, but garden-variety plastic planters rolling around in geranium-filled mud puddles. Assuming they weren't being truly tossed, we picked them up and examined them on the way to stowing them at the owners' garage, lest they blow away completely.

Seeing some lighting potential in plastic planters, we scouted them out at the local garden center. A few months later we designed a shop in New York where we put them all together, two urns each with their tops bolted together, their bottoms recycled, and all suspended with custom coiled retractile cord.

THIS PAGE: The lamps
illuminated in the shop

tools & supplies

- drill
- ¼" drill bit
- electrical retractile cord
- three 1x¼" bolts
- three ¼" wing nuts
- lamp cord
- socket
- thin wire
- lightbulbs
- ceiling hook
- anchor
- hose clamp

step 1

Remove the base of the planter; it just pulls off and recycle it. Drill three ¼" holes, evenly apart, through the rim. These are for three 1" bolts with wing nuts. Make sure the holes are not close to any plastic ridges that will get in the way of the wing nuts. Match the second planter to the rim, and drill the matching holes. Drill a hole through the exact center of the top plate, and then three holes around that, for ventilation.

step 2

Put one end of the lamp cord through new hole at the top of the planter, through a bolt a little larger than the cord, and assemble a socket as shown in Basic Wiring, (page 138). The planters are not heavy, so a knot in the cord can support them without strain. However, you want the cord to swag, which is the reason for the bolt on the wire. A thin wire tied to this is what will support the whole fixture from the ceiling.

step 3

Test that the light works and close the planters to-gether; the bolts should go up through the bottom, with wing nuts down from the top, tightening the two planters together as one shape. Put an anchor in the ceiling or screw a hook into a joist. Suspend the planters from the wire on the ceiling hook. At about 12" up the wire, affix that length of stretched cord, with a tightened small hose clamp. Let the rest of the cord swag to either an outlet or another cord; sometimes a few draped lamps like this look nice together in the swooping form of a chandelier. Re-ally it's up to you as to what you want to do with the cord. Planters make equally nice floor lamps. When we made these in the shop, just resting upright or toppled over, lit up, with the great expanse of coiled cord, they were really great looking.

basic wiring

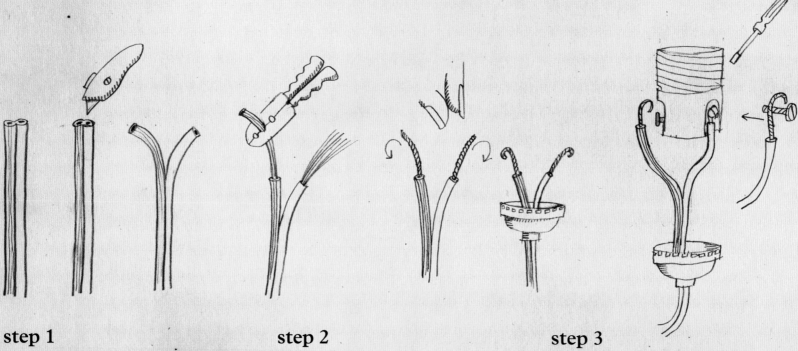

step 1

An average lamp cord is two plastic-covered wires connected side by side. There is a striped wire with ridges in the plastic, and another wire in solid smooth plastic. The striped wire is the live one, while the solid wire is neutral. Sometimes these will also be black and white, black being the live wire.

step 2

With a razor, separate the two plastic sides. Be careful not to veer off into the actual copper wire in the center of the plastic. Peel the two sides apart. With wire strippers, strip off about an inch of plastic from each wire. The "wire" is really a bundle of super-thin little wires, so you need to twist these between your fingers into one braid.

step 3

Slip the cord through the lamp socket's stem and socket cap, and curl the ends of the wires so they'll fit around the terminal screws. The brass screw is hot and takes the striped wire, while the silver screw is neutral and gets the solid wire. Loop them around the screws clockwise. Tighten the screws.

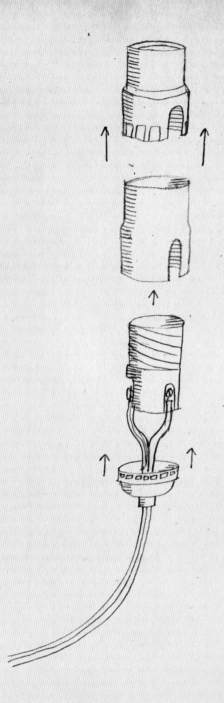

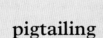

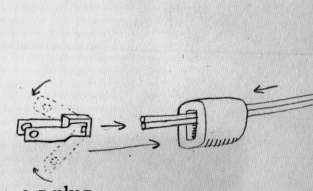

step 4

Now everything fits together: the cardboard insulator slips over the socket body and the socket cap snaps into the outer shell

pigtailing

Pigtailing is connecting two or more cords to a cord that will go to the outlet. For example, if you wanted to make a chandelier with five lights, you'd pigtail three of those cords to one cord, then the other two to another cord, then those two cords get pigtailed to one cord that ends with a plug. Just make sure all the stripes go together and all the solids go together and never the twain shall meet.

e-z plug

Simple "e-z" plugs are found at the hardware store. Slip the plug housing over the end of the cord, then open the prongs and press the plug onto the cord. Close the prongs into the plug, then tightly press the plug into the housing.

decorative
140-209

decorative

Decorative is a word we use to describe anything where an attempt has been made at injecting an aesthetic into it.

Of course that attempt has been made in every other section, but they all had a common theme.

This section, however, runs the gamut; it includes faux mantels, faux pine needles, faux clumps of grass, real clumps of grass, and real clump of trees. We've also attempted little injections of personalization: monogramming a rug and the head of a key, etching "bespoke" lip prints on a glass, and initialing wall molding and a mantel. We even turn wall molding into a mantel. As a yard sale ad would say, "something for everyone."

art base

This project started out as a way to give credit to objects that were considered unusable or worthless. Everybody has these things that make other people ask, "why do you still have this and what is it?" It could be a dented riding helmet, a broken camera lens, a piece of the Berlin wall, an umbrella handle, a handmade brick from deep inside Rockefeller Center, a corn-cob pipe—really anything at all. What they happen to share is that to anyone else but you, they look like garbage. In order to change that, they need to look as important as they are. In this case we had an Alvar Aalto "65" chair in an extremely weathered state of decay. In our eyes, this was a beautiful thing. More rare than an actual Aalto chair is one that's been beaten down by the weather so much that it's actually starting to come apart. And by coming apart it's showing how it's made, which is part of the beauty of it. But to anyone else it looks like garbage. We couldn't very well keep the entire thing on a cube, so we unscrewed the legs, which are the most important part of the design anyway. Without the base though, these would still look like kindling. But up on the base, even with all the dirt that came with them, the peeling varnish, and split birch, they look as special as they are.

RIGHT: The Aalto legs on their art base

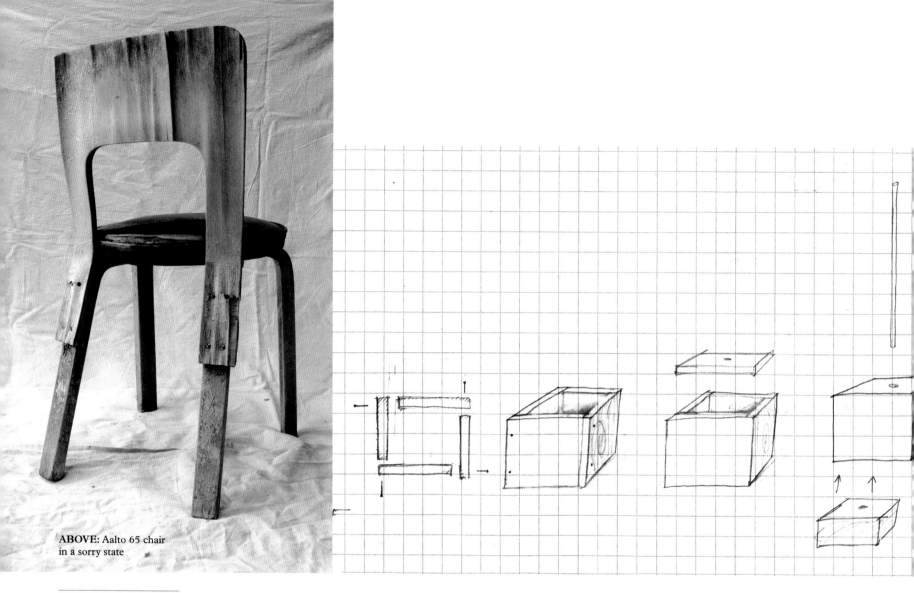

ABOVE: Aalto 65 chair in a sorry state

tools & supplies

- scrap board more than ¼" thick
- saw
- wood glue
- 1½" finishing nails
- sandpaper
- ½" dowel
- ½" drill bit
- scrap 2x4" wood
- mallet
- pebbles
- plaster or cement mix
- drill
- paint
- Velcro (optional)

step 1

First you need to find a piece of ¾" board. Ours was a scrap piece, probably from a construction site Dumpster. Other thicknesses will work, although ¼" is too thin; you need to be able to nail the four sides together at the edges. Cut four pieces the same width and the same height. The art base doesn't have to be a cube; it just has to look good with what you'll be putting on it. For example, for the Aalto legs, the base would look awkward if it was short and wide, because the "art" is vertical. However if we'd positioned the Aalto legs horizontally, then the base could have used a little more width, so two of the boards would be say, 8½" wide, and two would be 5" wide, but they'd all be the same height (e.g. 6").

step 2

Once the sides are cut, wood glue the edges to be joined and nail them together. We used 1½" finishing nails. It's easiest to set these into an edge first and then tap them into a perpendicular side edge, all around. Follow the diagram above. Now cut the top. You can either measure or trace the outline of the base onto a new board, and then cut it. Sand the edges smooth and glue/nail it onto the top of the four sides. You'll be supporting your art on a dowel, so now drill the appropriate-sized hole in the center of the top. For ours we used a ½" dowel, and drill bit.

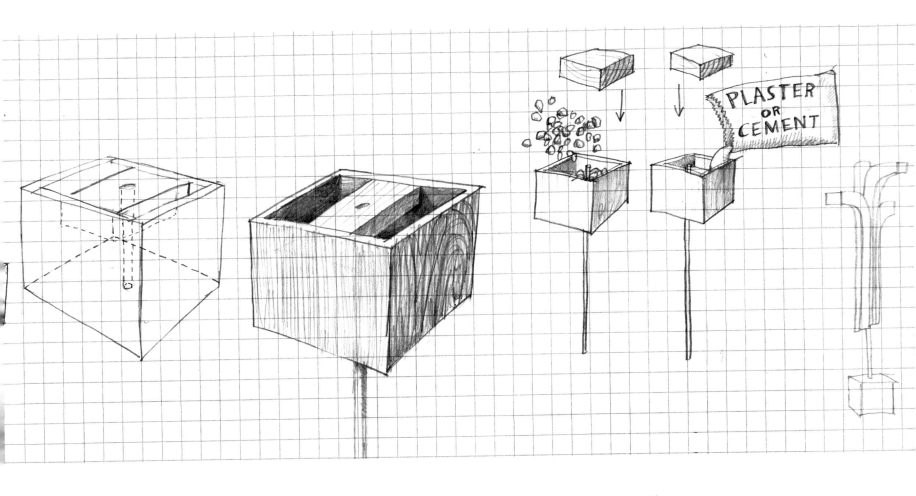

step 3

Now cut a chunk of 2x4" to fit into the underside of the base as shown in the diagrams above. Drill a hole in its center in order to hold the bottom of the dowel. Fit this new piece into the underside of the base, and then mallet the dowel in from the top. Now the 2x4" on the bottom should be centered, and the dowel for the top should be sturdy and straight. But whatever you put on the dowel could make the whole thing topple, so the base needs to be as heavy as possible.

step 4

Keep the base upside down and supported somehow—between the end of two flat-top sawhorses, tables, in a vice, in the umbrella hole of a table, a knothole, etc. Throw some everyday pebbles into the box, and then mix that with plaster or cement, up to the rim, covering the sides of the 2x4". Once this dries, your art base will be sturdy. Both plaster and cement require water and mixing, and they both dry quickly. There are different varieties, but in the end they all work well, especially for this job.

step 5

With the box dry and heavy, turn it upside down. You may want to add little felt pads on the bottom so you don't scratch any surfaces. Paint the base the desired color. Now the "art" goes on. For our Aalto legs, we drilled a ½" hole in the bottom of the "center" leg, but we didn't want to nail the legs together since somewhere down the line we may want to use them for a table. So we attached the legs together with Velcro, two opposing pieces on each leg.

tools & supplies

- boombox
- ipod
- Velcro
- 3.5 mm RCA cable

ipod boombox

This juggernaut of 1980s technology was in the backyard of the first tag sale Linda and I went to together. It was $9, and would've been more but the man said his son used to take it to the beach, so it was a little sandy to charge too much for. Happily we bought it, along with a Moulinex coffee grinder and a Lawrence Sanders paperback. You may think "big deal", but to us it was an absolutely auspicious beginning. The behemoth radio has been with us ever since, a fixture in the studio.

We've always preferred the look of a classic boombox over that of either a full-blown audio center or little separate components dispersed around a room, especially when it's mixed into a more formal setting, like a classics-filled bookcase, or sandwiched between a pair of Staffordshire dogs. Or I imagine it would look great in a yurt, or an igloo, or strapped to a Vespa. They're a really great piece of design that unfortunately many people think might have to be retired because of obsolescence. Luckily that's not the case. In fact we've only used the tape decks or the radio on ours a couple times, since its function is primarily to act as the amplifier speakers for an iPod, or the laptop, and look awesome. More awesome still, the iPod fits perfectly in the tape deck (you need to remove the tape deck door first, though). The diagram above shows how to revive your boombox, by using a simple 3.5mm-RCA audio cable. The RCA cable is the common split cord, one ending in red and the other in white. The 3.5mm end fits into the top of the iPod, or if you prefer the laptop, into the headphones jack.

We added the buffalo horns to ours, in a nod to Malcolm McLaren, but it came with "radio" painted on it (we're not that ironic).

eiffel mantel

Enzo Mari is an Italian designer notable for myriad fantastic designs, including "16 Animali," 16 wooden animals all intertwined in a jigsaw puzzle. In 1974 Mari wrote *Autoprogettazione*, roughly translated as "Self-made Projects," a book of furniture designs that anyone could make using the simplest lumber available at the hardware store. The lumber involved only 1x2" and 1x6" planks of the very common, off-the-rack, #2 (medium-grade) knotty yellow pine.

Gustave Eiffel was, of course, the renowned engineer of the Eiffel Tower. What the designer and engineer had in common was an economical way of building their respective projects, using no walls or big slabs of steel, and taking up virtually no mass.

We took our inspiration for the mantel from both men equally. From Mari, the raw pieces of wood are common 1x2" pine, found at any hardware store or lumberyard. (In our case we found them at a construction-site Dumpster, a fairly easy place to find them, adding one more facet to the economics of building with 1x2"s.) Also from Mari was the slapdash construction using a saw, hammer, and nails. From Eiffel we took the engineering—his basic x-i framework, which when we look at it technically, is really just beautiful scaffolding. The shape was taken from the Arc de Triomphe, which makes this this mantel a mélange of Parisian design, the Arc d'Eiffel, and Enzo Mari.

As Mari and Eiffel prove, the 1x2" is a three-dimensional manifestation of a line (assuming they drew their projects first); so if you have a pencil and a ruler, you can design just about anything. Our intention here was to design a graceful skeletal framework, like a box kite, and leave it at that. Possibly it would get surfaces made of Lucite (it actually still might, although this would put the kibosh on any economy). Our intention in ending construction at the framing point was to show the beauty of the "bones" of a mantel. This is the same idea as the The Visible Chair project (page 36). But whereas that could be construed conceptually as a view inside the "history" of a chair, this mantel idea doesn't live as far downtown.

When we finished our mantel it was immensely gratifying; after making this beautifully engineered structure we felt confident that we could now go ahead and build anything! The square with the x and the vertical piece just seemed like the absolutely perfect building block, which accounts for all the doodles of other ideas. A chair would be great looking, like an old club chair. The two desks I doodled look like the stage at a fairground, and if you were a concert promoter, or a roadie, this would be a great desk. The same goes with the bed, which might look great made from aluminum, powder coated a color. If you're really adventurous, you could attempt building on a larger scale with this engineering, creating your own house, with cantilevered sunroom and dock. Once you have a basic building module, the world is yours.

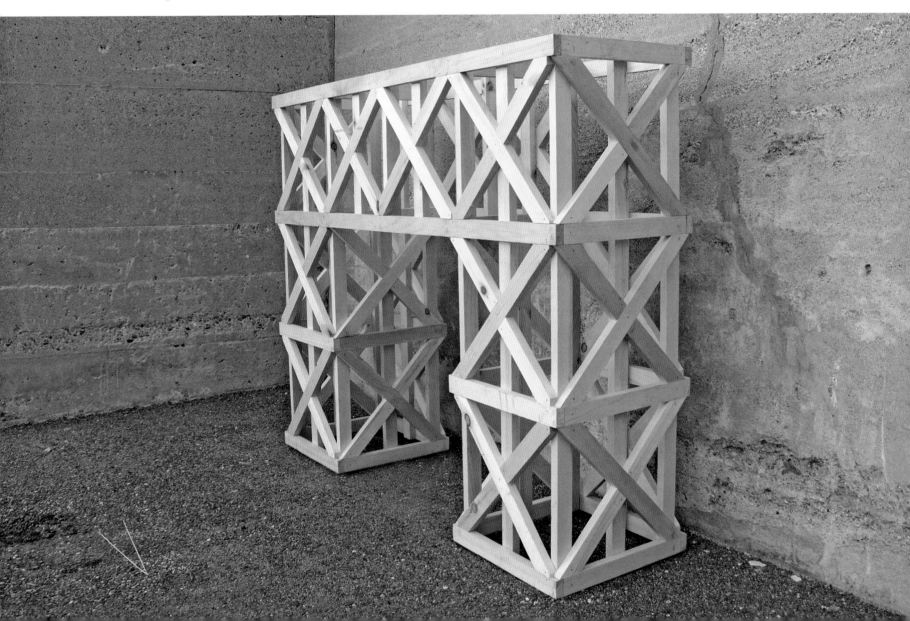

THIS PAGE: 1x2"s
at a construction site

step 1

All of the pieces are 1x2"s, which actually measure to be ¾x1½".

To start with, make two pieces as shown above; these will be the front and the back. The top piece of the mantel measures 53¼"; you'll need four of these: two on the top, front and back, and two 12" below those.

step 2

The legs, or corners of the columns, measure 42". You'll need eight of these right now, but cut 16. Put the top 53¼" piece on the ground, and nail the edges of the 42" pieces into its flat side, starting the first one ¾" away from the end, the second one 12" away from that, and the other two the same way. Nail another 53¼" piece 12 inches down from the first one, parallel to it. See the photos for assistance. Do this again to make the other side.

step 3

Once you've made these two sides, the rest is much easier. Next, cut 16 pieces at 13½" long; these will connect the front to the back, starting at the top, then the next one down is 12" away, then another 12", then another, which is across the bottom. So you should end up with 12" of height between each section. Do this for the outside of the other column, then the insides.

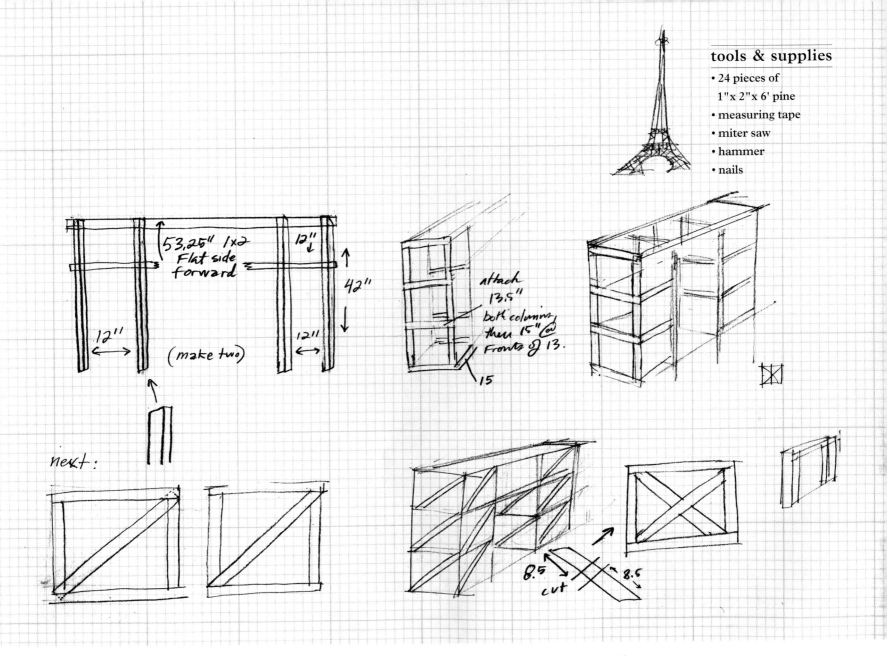

step 4

Now take the remaining eight 42" pieces and put them down the centers of each column, flat side facing out, and nail them in from the inside. (This is easier than it sounds.)

step 5

Cut eight pieces at $14\frac{7}{8}$" long. These are sections "b," and they go across the middle and bottom of each column, overlapping the ends of the $13\frac{1}{2}$"-long pieces.

Now cut 6 pieces at 15" each. These go on the top lintel. The one in the middle is nailed in with its edge forward, while the two on either side are nailed in with their flat side forward.

step 6

Cut 52 pieces to $18\frac{5}{8}$". On the ends of these, cut 45° angles, so the front view looks like a parallelogram (you're cutting these across the 2" face, not the 1" edge). Nail the first 26 of these into the 12" square spaces on the mantel. The remaining 26 now need a $1\frac{1}{2}$" notch cut out of their midsection. You could put each one bisecting up against the newly nailed 26 and make a pencil mark on either side, or you could clamp a piece of wood on the saw to help make all the cross-cuts even. We did the former, but the latter is definitely possible. When those are cut, nail them onto either side of the first diagonal piece.

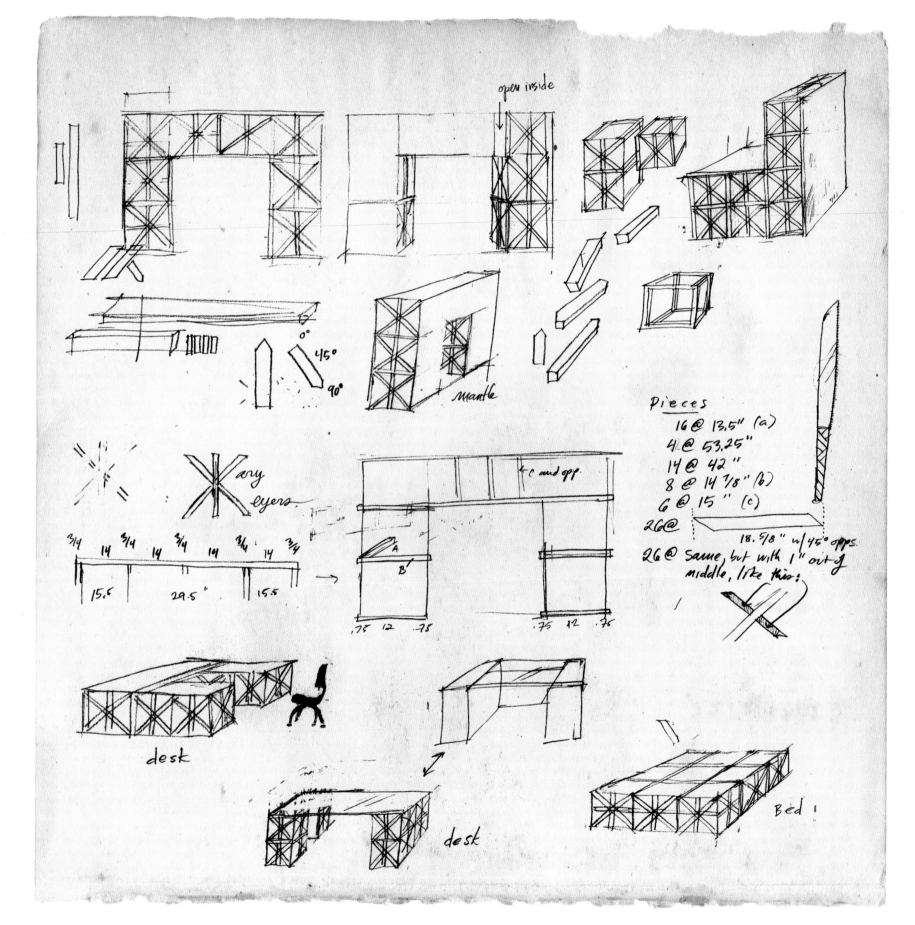

open inside

mantle

Xary eyers

¾ 14 ¾ 14 ¾ 14 ¾ 14 ¾

15.5   29.5"   15.5

0°
45°
90°

← c and opp.

A
B

.75 12 .75   .75 12 .75

Pieces
16 @ 13.5" (a)
4 @ 53.25"
14 @ 42"
8 @ 14 7/8" (b)
6 @ 15" (c)
26@
18.5/8" w/ 45° opps.
26 @ same, but with 1" out of middle, like this:

desk

desk

Bed!

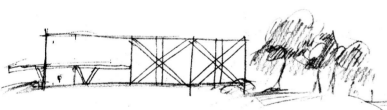

That should be it. For the top, you could either repeat the squares, cutting more diagonals and cross pieces to create a surface, or cut 3 pieces of ½x5-½x61" pine board and lay them on the top. As we mentioned before, the most ideal top would be the ⅜" Lucite encasement, flush against all walls of the mantel. A compromise is to use a 15½x59½" sheet of glass. This will give you a practical surface, while letting light through, and let all the craftsmanship be visible.

1x2 molding

Wall moldings are not easy to come by. Houses built in the past 100 years most likely don't have them. They may have a chair rail, but big panels defined by half-round or square moldings are, sadly, a rarity these days, as they probably fell victim to cost effectiveness, or else popular taste. Moldings were great devices to break up vast areas of uninteresting wall. Of course you could always hang art, shelving, wallpaper, or a giant mirror panels, but in this case we'll make molding.

Along with endless scraps of wood and building materials, 1x2" pieces of pine can be found in just about any construction-site Dumpster. They can be used to make myriad designs, as they're basically a three-dimensional straight line. So whatever you can draw with a ruler, you can make. And because it's from the Dumpster, it's not only free, but you're sparing the environment as well. The photos here are examples in two apartments of how we took scrap 1x2"s and made simple moldings. Opposite was for a French girl's apartment, and we designed them to resemble an Yves Saint Laurent Parisian airie. On the following page are simply stylized Orientalist moldings for a Japanophile graphic designer. So the paneled type molding need not be all Victorian fussiness. In these cases we're using them as graphic elements, with the resident's specific taste in mind. To that end, on the final page there's an illustration of ideas for molding, including an alphabet if you wanted to make panels that are specifically custom. Even though they're letters, that's not immediately obvious—they look more like a decorative graphic, and it's all the more rewarding when you point out the cleverness of your custom molding. At the top of the page are Cyrillic and Japanese characters. You can also put the 1x2"s on the wall sideways, to give the molding extra depth; or if don't want panels, you can just do a door frame. Define a headboard area, or as in the French dresser project, use 1x2"s as drawer pulls, or as a chair rail across a wall, or on a plain screen door from the hardware store, or caulked onto your windows as a decorative motif. A fun idea is to go around your house with your finger in the air "drawing" lines on things. Soon you'll be inspired.

tools & supplies

- 1x2" wood pieces
- sandpaper (100-, 200-, 400-grit)
- wood block
- damp rag
- oil primer
- oil paint
- paintbrush
- level
- pencil
- 2" finishing nails
- drill (optional)
- hammer
- spackle or plastic wood

ABOVE: Priming in progress
LEFT: A basic Chinoiserie design
OPPOSITE: Alphabet ideas
including Japanese and Cyrillic

step 1

First, the wood needs to be sanded. Do this with sandpaper wrapped around a block of wood and kept level with the 1x2", try not to slip off an edge. First sand with a 100 grit, then 200, then finish with 400. Wipe off any sanding dust completely with a damp rag. Let dry.

Paint the 1x2"s with an oil-based primer. No need to prime the side that will be against the wall as it obviously won't be showing.

Once the oil primer is dry it should look nice and smooth.

Paint the 1x2"s with oil paint on the three sides that will be showing. Oil paint is far superior to latex for painting things like molding and furniture in general. It goes on smoothly, evenly, and is less likely to leave brush marks; in fact it really doesn't leave brush marks at all. Oil seems to settle into itself and find its own level, likely because it takes a while to dry.

step 2

On the opposite page we've drawn some ideas for customized molding. You could follow these (they're out of scale, but figure each piece is 1x2" by the relative scale and length of a letter) or make up your own.

Cut the designs out with a chop saw, to be perfectly square, or a hand saw—pine cuts quickly, and if you mess up an angle you can always fill it with plastic wood later.

step 3

Have a level handy, and map out where the molding will be. Make sure you measure and space out the entire wall first. If you can, even draw it first on graph paper, although I find that sometimes it's easier just to eyeball something. Get everything out of the way and lean the long pieces up against the wall. When they look good, make a mark on the wall, but then measure to get the right height from the floor/ceiling. This is usually a little higher off the floor than down from the ceiling.

Nail it up to the wall using 2" finishing nails. If your wall gives you trouble, like the plaster chips as soon as a nail touches it, you need to drill pilot holes (narrower than the nail). What helps here is to have someone hold them plumb while you drill or nail at least two holes, so it stays in place. Hammer the finishing nails in at different angles, this will make the molding sturdier.

Once it's all nailed to the wall, go back and set all the nails deeper into the molding. You can easily do this with another nail, just tapped with a hammer onto the head of the nail in the molding. These holes you'll need to fill with a little spackle or plastic wood, let dry, sand, and then touch up with the oil paint. Or, chances are you won't even notice the nails if you just go around with a tiny brush and touch up the nail heads without setting them in deeper.

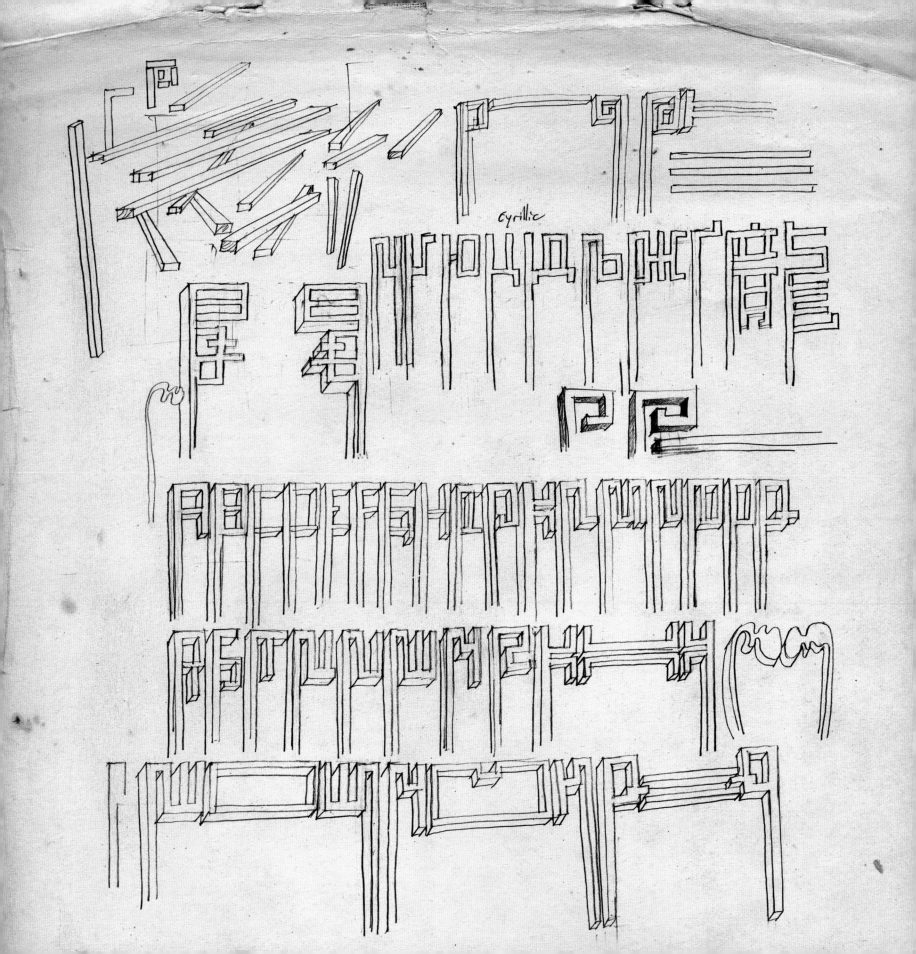

Cyrillic

wine cork

tools & supplies

- driftwood or branch
- knife

We found this burl of wood on a Maine island, and at the time I thought it was cork, or better yet old grape vine. It turns out it was probably just a knot of pine driftwood, but the idea to make our own wine bottle stoppers was already plugged into my mind. With a little precision whittling they may not be impermeable, but they do have a fresh-from-the-vineyard (of an eccentric Tuscan) feel to them and I imagine that all clustered together they would look like the grand cru at the drink table of a dinner party. Any old gnarled branch will do, and you can whittle using virtually any sharp knife. We tried to form the "stopper" of ours into a finger, but if you achieve a basic round shape you've succeeded.

tools & supplies

- Astroturf
- scissors
- sewing machine
- heavy duty thread
- large needle
- stuffing

astroturf pillows

We made these pillows as a seating pile for our porch, so it would seem as if we're out lounging around in the grass. They're made of a type of Astroturf, which is synthetic grass and therefore needs no mowing or watering—in fact water just rolls right off, so they're ideal for leaving outside. They're great for inside too, especially in a city, where a roll in the grass isn't always an option. In its original incarnation this was a mat from a deli, tossed in a Dumpster because it was too thick and customers were tripping.

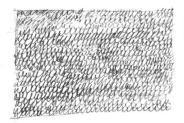

step 1

Lay out the mat to see how much material you have to work with. Cut the turf into strips the width you want your pillow, then cut twice the length of the pillow. Fold the material so the "grass" is on the inside.

step 2

Stitch the three sides almost closed—leave an opening for the stuffing. Pull the pillow outside in, with the "grass" now on the outside and stuff the inside with anything—we used old rags and some poly fill. Stitch closed.

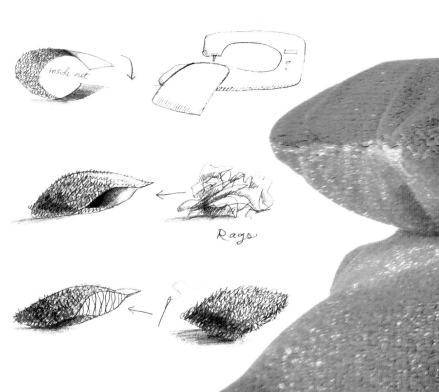

flotsam
door
handle

tools & supplies

- flotsam
- drill
- ½" titanium bit
- 60-grit sandpaper
- steel-wood epoxy
  (Liquid Nails)
- ⅝x1" hex bolts
- rachet

Walking on Long Island, Maine one day, we couldn't help but notice a giant sofa in a clearing by the water. An early 1970s plaid sleeper, it looked as if it'd been sloshing around the rec room of the briny deep for the last 30 years. One nice casualty of this was the exposed wood wings, once were probably a rich dark brown lacquer, but now were stripped, silvered, and worn smooth. It was only later we thought what a great door handle it would make, as we were in the process of designing a shop in New York City. So it was back to the island the next morning armed with a useless drill against the sofa's saltwater rusted screws. If you attempt an operation like this bring a full tool kit, saw and all. Or else like me, you'll be stuck with only an axe from a nearby tree stump in an early morning battle with the far-too-well-made leviathan.

LEFT/Long Island, Maine
OPPOSITE: New York City

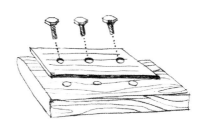

step 1

If you can remove the existing steel handle, you can put the flotsam on with any u-bracket or customized elbow bracket, but in our case the handle didn't come off. So, you need to drill toward the glass door. Make sure you have a block of wood protecting the glass. Drill three staggered holes into the steel door handle with a ½" titanium tipped drill bit. Put the flotsam onto the front of the steel handle, and from the other side, mark the flotsam with a pen through the holes. At these points, drill a ½" hole into the wood, but not all the way through.

step 2

Scruff up the steel surface with 60-grit sandpaper. Coat the steel handle and the flotsam connections with a steel-wood epoxy. Ratchet in three ⅝x1" hex bolts through the back side of the steel handle to the inside of the flotsam. You shouldn't have any screws showing through the wood, or else it loses its grace, hence the necessity of bolting through the back, and using the epoxy.

initialed rug

tools & supplies

- rug
- charcoal stick
- box cutter
- Kool-Aid
- large pot of water
- Gorilla Glue or
  heavy-duty glue

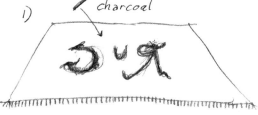

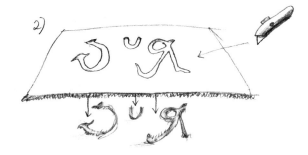

This is another personalization idea. This time thanks go to Julian Schnabel and his carpet for the lobby of the Gramercy Park Hotel, which was inspired by a fragment of an old Spanish rug. It's not a new idea, putting a logo or a club's seal on a carpet, but the way it's done, the custom typeface used, the kerning of the letters, and the history and elegance behind it are what elevates it above a mere welcome mat. In our case, we pilfered Schnabel's typeface, took our own 5x7' shag rug, cut out the initials r, u, and g, dyed them in Kool-Aid, and glued them back in.

step 1

Draw the letters on a piece of paper, to practice first. When you have what you like, turn the rug over, and use a stick of charcoal to draw the letters on, backwards.

step 2

Using a box cutter, cut the letters out; twist the rug to look at the shag side, and make sure you're not cutting through pile, but rather just the backing. If you do lose some pile, keep it to glue on later.

Pick up the cut-out letters and keep them in a pile.

step 3

We dyed the letters in Kool-Aid, which produces beautiful, saturated colors. Use about 20 packets of unsweetened Kool-Aid for every pound of fabric (the letters should be only about a pound). Use a big enamel pot with water enough to cover the letters, pour in the Kool-Aid (don't get it on anything but the inside of the pot and the letters), mix it around, put it on the stove top, and bring it to a near boil. Let it cool and then use warm water to rinse. Let it hang dry, and don't wring it out.

step 4

When the letters are dry, turn the rug over face down; then place the newly dyed initials back in place. You can use any heavy-duty glue to seal the back of the rug into place again. When the glue sets, turn the rug over and fluff up any little shag pieces, and precisely glue in the stray pieces that may have fallen out earlier.

lip print glasses

One day we were at a giant discount store and noticed rows and rows of really nice German glassware, perfectly plain. In a sense these were "tossed," in that nobody wanted them at the full-price store, so we could turn them into a project. They were the perfect blank canvas for a customized project, and our first thought was to use etching cream and brush on a monogram. But we already had a set of antique glasses with an "M" etched on them from my grandfather. As much as we could make a more updated initial or monogram, the thought of making the truly personalized mark of lip prints seemed much more fun.

Painted-on etching cream would create that even, frosted finish, and look nearly the same as a sandblasted finish. There's no need to carve into the glass anyway, since this is based on a smear. We bought a set of the glasses, took them home and etched them, washed them, and dried them. Sitting on the table, they looked eerily almost as if we were either having or just had a party or company, sort of like the cardboard cutouts in the Steve Martin movie *The Lonely Guy*. Of course there are plenty of options as to what to "etch" on a glass—you could also try your hand at fingerprints.

tools & supplies

• drinking glasses
• etching cream
• small paintbrush

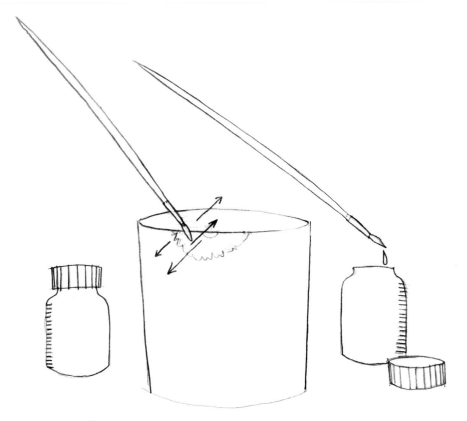

step 1

The best way to see a template is to put on some lip balm and take a pretend drink from a clear glass. This will give you a good plan of how to brush on the etching cream. With that glass in front of you, brush plain water in a lip print shape on a piece of paper, just for practice. After you've done that, brush the etching cream on a "scrap" drinking glass until you get the hang of it. You can't erase etching cream, so the first time you brush it on, it's permanent. Practice a little beforehand and you won't ruin your glasses.

step 2

Dip the brush into the etching cream so that half the bristles are covered. Brush the cream on the glass in back and forth diagonal strokes, the same direction as the creases in lips. Be liberal in the amount you brush on, but don't glob it on so thickly as to brush past the edges of your design. If you can, leave a couple slivers of lip crease, for realism. But don't be too realistic—the lip print should be more of a graphic design and have a certain amount of fun in it.

step 3

Once you've brushed on the design, wait about five minutes before rinsing it off. Hold the glass underwater upside down so the cream rinses off the rim and not down the glass. You may find that there is a little streaking and splotching. The streaking is okay, as long as it's going in the right direction, but if it's splotched, brush on more cream in that spot, back and forth, following the same technique. You can always touch them up, but you can't go backward, so be careful. Again, wait about five minutes before rinsing. Once they all look good, wash them like you'd normally wash a glass.

piggy doorstop

A few years ago we were in a house in Florida and noticed the screen door being held open by a cinderblock wrapped in a fluorescent t-shirt. That may sound bad, but at least there was an attempt at the decoration of a utilitarian object, which is always good. I think the charm was in the t-shirt, dressing up the concrete block with a "splash of color." These doorstops, in concrete or brick, aren't a new idea, but usually they're floral patterned, gingham cotton, or needlepoint, or they're stuffed with sand, in the shape of a cat or a duck. So, taking inspiration from all these incarnations, we thought we'd try to make one look a little more posh, but still have it serve no other purpose than to decoratively hold open a door. We used a knockoff Louis Vuitton duffle bag, a rock, some old t-shirts (an homage to Florida), and a wire. Unfortunately, we didn't have this book, otherwise we would've added a custom painted stripe (see page 82).

tools & supplies

- fabric or vinyl
- scissors
- sewing machine
- large needle
- thread
- old t-shirts or rags
- rock
- 12-gauge wire

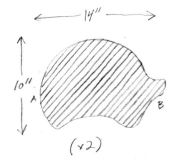
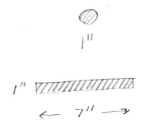
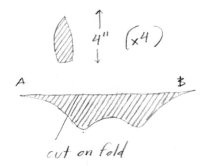

step 1

We sketched out different pigs, and attempted to make ones that would rival Steiff, but drafting a pattern for a stuffed animal isn't easy, so we finally settled on this rather triangular piggy.

First, draw a simple pig shape, or copy and enlarge the one above. The one thing that's crucial with an animal pattern is that the underneath pattern (the pork belly) lines up with the outer patterns. The way to assure this is to cut out one outer pattern and have the others match that.

step 2

Enlarge and cut the other patterns out, or make your own underneath pattern by folding a piece of fabric between the two outer patterns, so the fold is straight across from under the nose to the tail, as in the sketch. Cut this folded piece along the bottom, following the legs and belly. With a ½" seam allowance, cut these three pieces out of fabric or vinyl, and stitch them together on a sewing machine,

inside out. You'll end up with the nose hole, but also leave a flap, like a pair of long johns open in the back to fill the pig with stuffing, which includes a rock. Turn the pig inside out.

step 3

Hand stitch the snout on, and stuff the pig from the back, filling the snout first. We used cut up t-shirts and various rags, and pushed them into the snout with a stick. Keep a steady pressure up into the snout as the stuffing has a tendency to slip out into the body. You can use anything stuffing you want, but it needs to be a little more substantial than poly fill. When we were about halfway, we put a somewhat heavy (3 lbs. or so) rock inside, surrounded by more rags.

step 4

Make the tail by sandwiching a 12-gauge wire between two flaps of fabric or vinyl. Stitch the wire

completely inside, so there's no chance of it slipping out. Coil the tail around your finger once or twice. When the pig is stuffed full, stitch the back flap closed by hand, fitting and stitching the tail in place as well. One or two stitches should be fine, but you could use a drop or two of hot glue, or if you're using vinyl, an epoxy made for vinyl.

step 5

Cut four pieces of the same shape for the ears. We used the Vuitton pattern for the outsides, or the back, of the ears, and a caramel color for the insides of the ears. The caramel vinyl was on the inside of the duffle bag. The ears don't require any stuffing or turning inside out, so just stitch them closed. Attach them to the body by a couple of stitches at either end of the base of the ear.

painted radiator

Like many people, we looked at junkyards or architectural salvage yards with the same question: why so many radiators? Later we understood that radiators are just like any other piece of furniture, but weighing hundreds of pounds and requiring professional removal and installation. So this is a *Tossed & Found* project wherein the first part may require a qualified radiator installer. But the second part is more fun and anyone can do it. Firstly, you may already have a radiator. If you do that's great, but bear in mind that they can be changed out with another radiator which you may like better. Be armed with a photo of your existing radiator and maybe you could work out a trade. Or at least the salvage yard can see what you're offering. Of course, that's only if you want to trade up. The second part of this project involves painting the radiator. It's a myth that they need to be painted silver or white. Silver and metallic paints actually hinder heat transmission, and white paint can yellow and show rust quicker than any other color. As shown opposite, radiators can be painted any color. In this case, we wanted it to look a bit like an old Le Creuset cast-iron pot, but more exaggerated. I think a rainbow paint job would look great in a monochromatic room.

ABOVE: At the salvage yard

tools & supplies

- radiator
- wire brush
- chemical paint
- stripper (optional)
- rags
- oil-based primer
- paintbrush
- 1 to 2 quarts oil paint

step 1

Clean your radiator to a fare-thee-well. If there's any loose paint, use a wire brush. You may also need to use a chemical paint stripper if your radiator has that rounded paint look on any relief work, or you may not want to bring out the filigreed metal work, which is fine. Brush on an oil-based primer with a heavier concentration of zinc chromate (this is a rust and corrosion impeder). The hardware store sells radiator brushes, if you find it hard to get down the back. One coat of primer should be fine.

step 2

If you want to do a gradient like ours, you'll need to buy two quarts of paint: one yellow and one orange. The far right section is pure yellow, and the far left is pure orange. Begin meeting the twain by adding a little orange to the yellow and vice versa. We suggest mixing up your gradients in clear plastic drinking cups before painting, as things could go awry by overcompensating one column and undercompensating another.

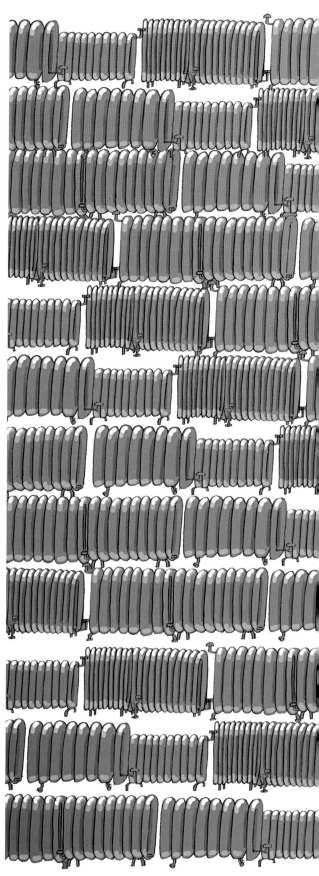

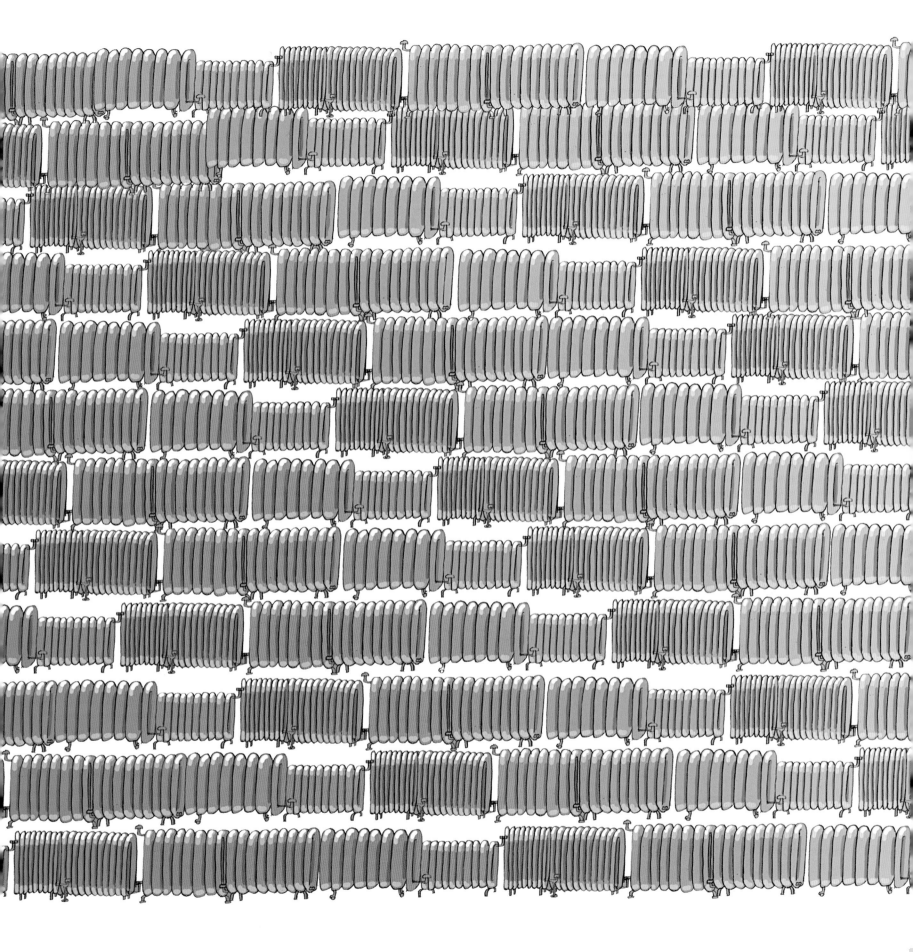

pine needle sachet

One knickknack that pops up fairly often at yard sales in Maine is the souvenir balsam pine–scented sachet. It's usually just a square cotton pillow stuffed with ground-up pine tree and printed with a nature scene. You can put them in a dresser drawer, in the car, on the coffee table—it's an *objet*. One day while thinking about what to make people for a holiday gift, we thought we'd make one of our own. At first it was going to be in the form of a little tree stump, or a puffy version of a rearview mirror tree.

Then we thought about the perfectly simple shape of the pine needle itself, and designed the sachet like one, but just enlarged the scale. All together in a pile they would look like the floor under an unwatered Christmas tree, and smell just as nice. We used wool from a local mill that had unfortunately closed production, but still had a surplus, and the balsam was originally from a couple of bags from yard sales, and when that ran out we found more at the local hardware store.

ABOVE: Sachets at yard sales

tools & supplies

• dark green wool
• sewing machine
• matching thread
• balsam
• needle

step 1

Cut the wool into two large 10½" pine needle shapes, as seen opposite. If there is a better side to the wool, put this on the inside, so it will be on the outside when you turn it inside out.

step 2

Sew a ¼" seam allowance all around the perimeter, but leave a space of about 4" open.

Turn the needle inside out, so the good side is now outside. If it's difficult to pull the points out, use the end of a paintbrush, chopstick, or skewer to get the clogged fabric into its pointed end. Don't push too hard or you'll poke a hole in the end of the wool.

step 3

Stuff the needle with balsam; keep pushing it toward either end, and finish with stuffing in as much as you can in the middle. You can buy balsam from a craft shop or hardware store, especially in wintertime.

With a matching green thread, or at least matching the thread you used for the rest of it, hand stitch your pine needle closed. Ideally you'd make a hundred of these and put them underneath a big stuffed Charlie Brown—type Christmas tree.

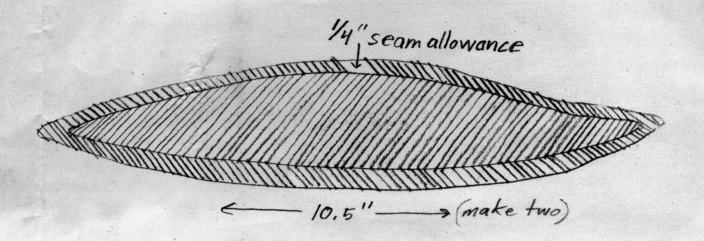

"¼" seam allowance

← ——— 10.5" ——— → (make two)

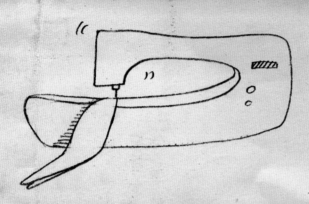

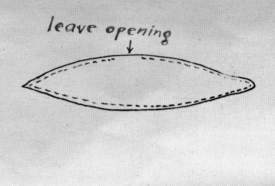

leave opening

turn inside-out

stuff with balsam.

stitch opening
closed

terrarium

tools & supplies

- jar with lid
- clear packing tape
- pebbles
- activated charcoal
- potting soil plus
  plants or seeds,
  or a piece of turf

A few years ago we bought a vintage hanging, lighted, glass terrarium at a barn sale. It was really great looking and we had the best intention to make a hanging *Road to Morocco*–type oasis, or a suspended bonsai circular boxwood maze, or even a regular terrarium. But in the end the proliferation of spider plants in our apartment made the terrarium idea become the odd man out. We still liked the idea, but it needed to be more casual, more natural. The look of 18th- and 19th-century naturalist specimen collections has always appealed to us, and even though the specimens were usually dead or preserved, the glass cloches were the real draw. So as it turns out, the perfect solution to our terrarium dilemma was staring us in the face from the recyclable bin. A natural, unplanned, botanist's specimen–type planting inside would be just the right harmonious accompaniment, like a diorama about the good of recycling. We went to the forest and brought back a clump of turf—a little mound of moss with some odds and ends and grasses springing from it. When we put it on some pebbles on the underside of the lid, it was a little tricky to get the lid on, so we made a looped tube of clear tape to act as "edging." This cleared the dirt and pebbles out of the way of the lid's grooves, and now we could also build up the base of pebbles a little higher, so the moss would clear the curved distortion of the jar.

The day after we screwed the lid closed, the jar was filled with condensation, looking like it had rained inside, then it cleared up, and did the same the next day, and the next, and so on. We had created the perfect recycled ecosystem.

step 1

Wash and dry the jar and lid. Take a piece of packing tape and roll it in a circle, slightly less wide than the diameter of the inside of the lid, with the sticky side facing out, and place it on the underside of the lid, which is facing up. This now gives you a base on which to put the rest of the ingredients.

step 2

The first layer is pebbles—nothing special, we picked ours from the driveway. The pebbles will act as an aerated space for the water to dry and not rot, which is what happens when you plant things in pots with no holes in the bottom. Use a rather tall ¾" of pebbles in order to build up a little height so the little details in the moss won't be distorted.

step 3

The next layer is activated charcoal, which is the kind of pure, aquarium charcoal that acts as an air filter and keeps things fresh—especially important in this closed environment.

step 4

The potting soil is next, and any plants or seeds. Or you could put in a little piece of the woods, which is what we did.

Water the plants, making sure the soil is damp; this will be the last time you water it, unless it looks like it's dying, of course.

With all of these things resting on the inside of the lid, gently fit the glass over the plants. Screw it closed tightly and keep in area with partial sunlight.

LEFT: ecosystem growing
inside a pickle jar

boro jean quilt

Boro is a Japanese word that means "rags" or "tattered clothes." The word usually refers to a type of recycled indigo denim resourcefully used and reused by poor Japanese peasants, farmers, and fisherman, who can't afford the luxury of new cloth. Repeated patching and mending of denim with other denim resulted in odd designs, layers of history, and pieces of generations. Fishing and mosquito nets were also repaired this way, using a combination of netting, indigo cotton, rags, and thread. There's a beauty of craft stitched into these utilitarian boro mendings—a "beautility."

Imagine owning a pair of jeans for years and years, and all the patching that would be involved. And if the denim you were using to patch them was catch-as-catch-can, imagine what that would look like. After some years it would seem that the original denim wasn't even a factor anymore, and that your jeans were just patched squares. We're not making a pair of jeans, but that's the idea behind our quilt, and boro is being economically resourceful with denim. Our boro is made from indigo denim and patched with blue jeans, some of which were ours, and others which were bought at the thrift store. We decided to turn it into a throw for the winter and applied quilted patches that read "home sweet home." The entire boro was then backed with a large piece of Day-Glo floral cotton and stuffed again.

You could of course also use boro made of khaki, wool, Indian blankets, camouflage, flannel—really anything, as a variation.

tools & supplies

- denim material 39x60"
- scrap denim jeans
- bleach
- rubber gloves
- pencil and paper
- batting
- scissors
- pins
- backing fabric
- sewing machine
- thread
- needle

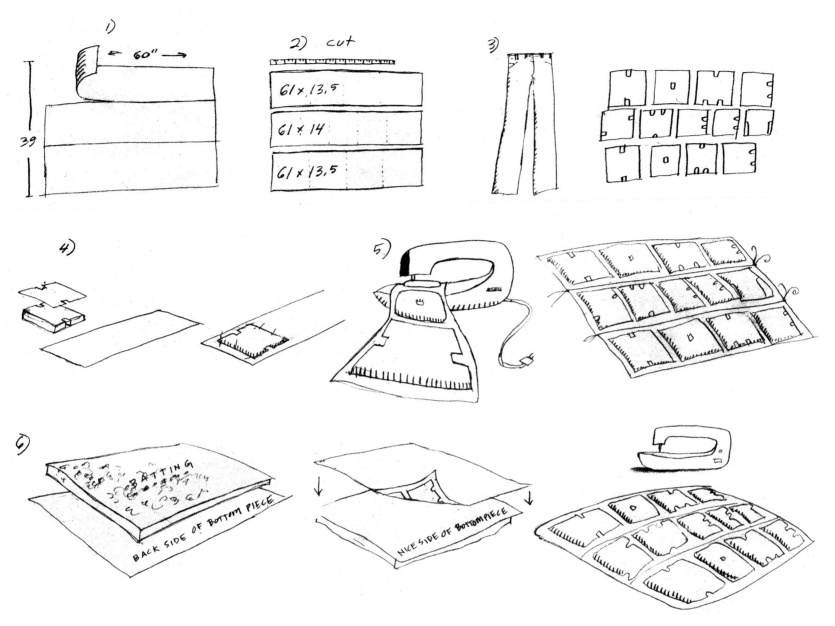

step 1

First, take a piece of denim and cut it 39x60". Unless you can find a piece this big handed down in a sufficiently boro state, you'll have to buy a new one from the fabric store. Or you could cut up blue jeans into a large pieces. The problem with that is you'll only get a few flat panels from each pair, and then the denim could be cut on the bias, giving you a rippled field.

step 2

Cut the denim into two strips measuring 61 x 13½" each (for the word "home" twice), and one piece at 61x14" (for "sweet"). To give these an aged look we put them in the washing machine with some bleach, each separately, with varying ratios of bleach to water. You can also do this in a bucket or a tub; just don't splash any bleach on yourself, and wear rubber gloves. Rinse the pieces out with soap and water and then dry them, and iron them.

step 3

The strips may have shrunken in the dryer, so put them together (but don't sew them) to see how big your letters should be, giving yourself ½" as a seam allowance for when you sew the backing on. Use a piece of paper to draw the letters and make a template, i.e., cut out an H, O, M, E, S, W, and T. Now take these paper letters and put them on your blue jean rags, trace them, and cut them out. Try to find the most interesting parts of the jeans, but stay away from pockets and rivets. Cut out enough of each letter to spell all the words.

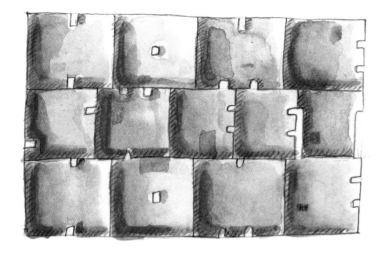

step 4

Put the denim letters on top of the batting; cut the batting about ½" in from the edges of the denim letters. When these are cut, spell out the words on each strip of denim, with the blue jean letters on top. Now pin each letter in place before you sew it.

step 5

Sew the letters to the backing with about ¼" seam allowance or as close to the edge as you can. Make sure the batting doesn't move around. Make sure to sew around the insides of the Os. Once the strips are done, stitch the three panels to one another.

step 6

Cut it a backing fabric the same size as the denim; this may be denim as well, or it may be anything else you want. Cut a piece of batting to match. Stitch the batting to the wrong side (not the side you want showing) of the backing fabric along the edges. Now lay the good side of the denim against the good side of the backing (see sketches) and stitch them together along the edges like a pillow, leaving the center of a smaller side open. Pull it inside out and hand stitch to close it up.

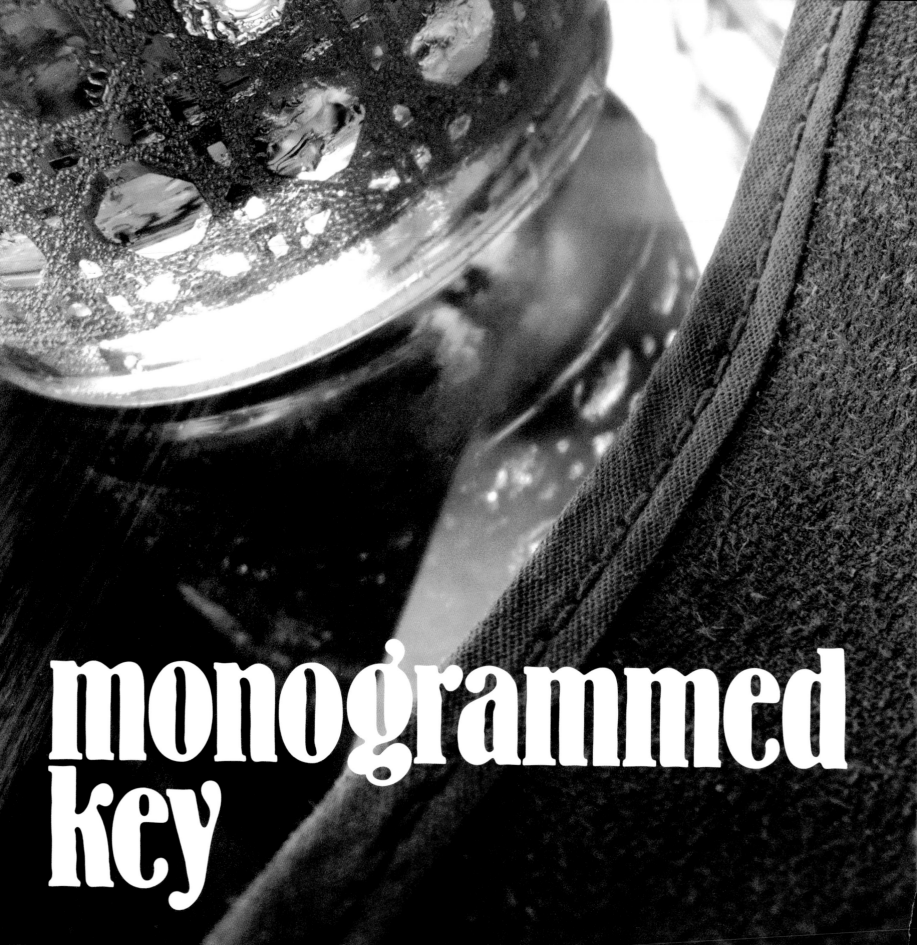

monogrammed
key

In a project akin to the Lip Print Glasses (page 168), when confronted with a vast wall of anonymous sameness, the tendency is to think about what will make you stand out as an individual. In this case it's a key, and while it's not a true found-on-the-side-of-the-road "tossed" object, it is an offshoot of thinking about the monogramming of the glasses, combined with the skeleton chairs and the rug, and knowing the fact that anything can be jigsawed.

Everyone carries around keys and they all look basically the same. So if it's fairly easy to make yours unique, then why not do it? This is a great weekend project. You can make one key in a few hours, and just think how impressive a set of monogrammed keys would look tossed on a desk.

tools & supplies

- key
- masking tape
- pencil
- table vice
- clamp (optional)
- drill
- $1/32$" titanium bit
- $1/16$" titanium bit
- jeweler's saw
- narrow blades
- needle files
- emery cloth
- metal polish (such as Noxon 7)

step 1

First, design a monogram. We drew some ideas on the opposite page, but if your initials are none of these, trace the shape of your key head a few times on a sheet of paper and start doodling. Solid letters (positive) will look better than spatial letters (negative). Try block letters to start; they may end up being all you need, and they're a little easier to cut. Your key should be blank, as in the photo in the previous page. Take a piece or two of masking tape and press it hard and flat onto the key head. Pencil your design onto the tape.

step 2

Clamp the key into a table vice by its tail (the long part). Using a titanium drill bit, drill your pilot holes. You may need to attach a clamp onto the vice to steady your drill. On the opposite page, we used a $1/32$" bit to drill between the W and the K, and a $1/16$" bit under and to the right of the K. Ideally you'd use a drill press, or more ideally a laser cutter, but getting through this and making it with your hands will be much more satisfying than having a machine do the work. Insert the jeweler's saw blade into a pilot hole, then reconnect the blade to the saw.

step 3

Cut thin lines with the thickness of one blade, e.g., the space between the W and the K. The space under the K was more "formed" than "cut" with the blade. Be very deliberate. Between the K and the M we cut up straight along the M, then brought the blade back and up along the K until it connected and fell out. The exterior cuts will be much easier. For instance, the M was cut straight up the left leg of the M, then back down again; then cutting up the long diagonal to that point again allowed us to notch out the crook to the right of the middle point. If this all seems like too much work, you can always contact a jeweler and ask them if they'd cut it for you, since they're already set up with the proper saws, drills, and vices.

step 4

Once you've made all the cuts, peel the tape off. Now use the needle files to clean up the cuts and straighten the lines, if they need it. You can't fit a file down into a thin cut, so cut some strips of fine emery cloth to clean the inside slits, but don't let either the cloth or the files scratch the surface of the key. After it's all filed, polish it with something like a Noxon 7 metal polish on a cloth. Then you can have the tail grooved at any hardware store.

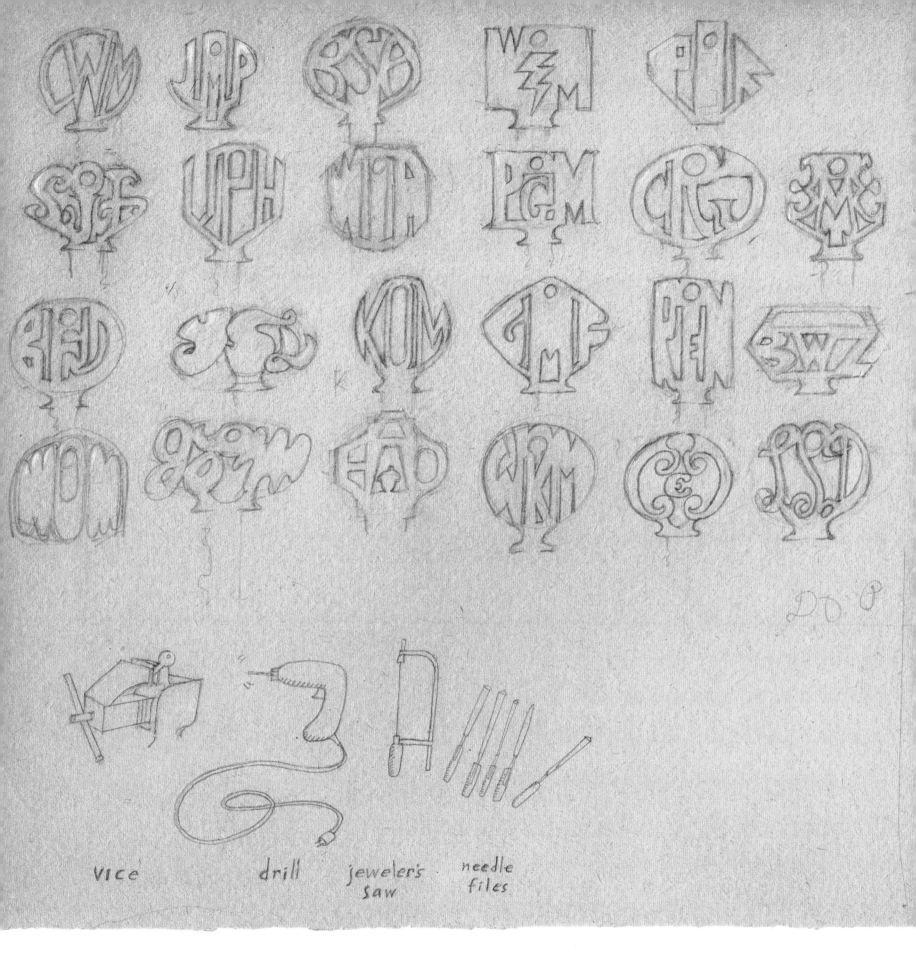

vice   drill   jeweler's   needle
                               saw   files

scrap wood mantel

Even if there's no fireplace inside, every home should have a mantel. It adds focus to a room, gives you a better sense of how to decorate, and creates the perfect spot for a painting, mirror, books, candlesticks, or something on an art base (see page 144). You could put faux burning logs inside and make it a great place for hanging out at parties or hanging stockings with care. Alternatively, you could put a television inside a mantel, use it for storage or to house speakers, turn the top lintel into a covered flip-down bar, or fold the whole thing down into a Murphy bed. The mantel is just a box, and boxes can become anything.

The aesthetic of a mantel is up to you. You might want something very sleek, like a white box, or traditional or very rustic, but either way you can build them for virtually nothing. In fact, if you looked in New York City construction-site Dumpsters for a week straight, you could probably find enough scrap wood to build your own house, with a mantel in every room.

On the page opposite and the following page, we've put together two "traditional" mantels, both from New York City scrap. The one opposite was compiled and built in a couple days. The lack of "polish" was an intentional aesthetic: if we had a piece of molding that was too short, like on the top, we used it anyway. The fact that it was built from scrap is something we wanted to celebrate. Interestingly, the photo of the mantel on the following page was taken in progress; later we painted it white. But I always thought it looked much better in its raw state, with the contrast of all the different woods. Our mistake was thinking that in order for something to look finished, it had to be painted, but by doing that sometimes you hide the creative ingenuity.

In order to make a basic mantel, gather as much wood as you can. Look especially in construction- or renovation-site Dumpsters. Keep in mind that these Dumpsters are used for scrap material to be hauled away, so they're a far cry from a Dumpster behind a restaurant. You may find coffee cups and crumpled aluminum foil from an egg and cheese sandwich, but that's about it—small inconvenience to pay in exchange for a new mantel. Construction-site Dumpsters are where you'll find the larger pieces: 2x4"s, 4x4"s, 2x10"s, sheets of plywood, panels of drywall

tools & supplies

- 2x4"s
- plywood
- screws
- saw
- decorative pieces

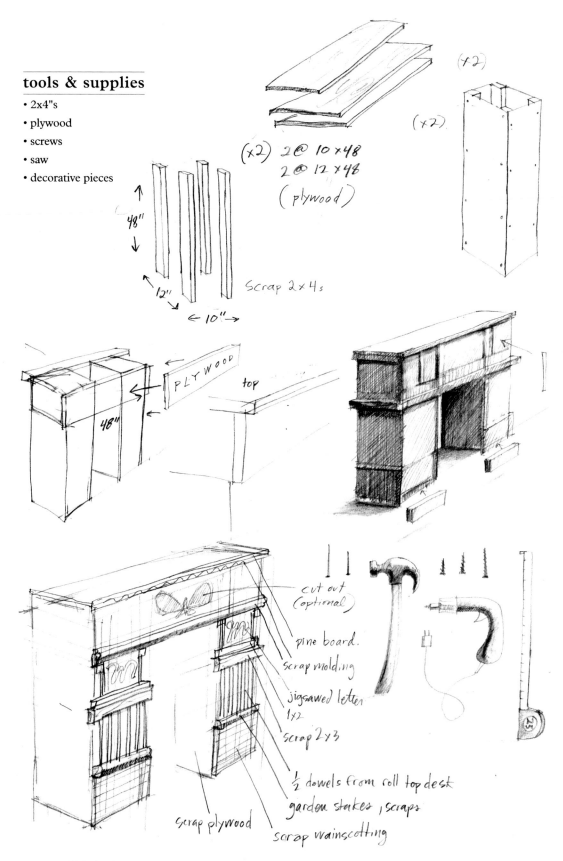

(x2)

(x2)

(x2) 2 @ 10 x 48
2 @ 12 x 48
(plywood)

48"

12"

← 10" →

Scrap 2x4s

PLYWOOD   top

48"

cut out (optional)

pine board.

scrap molding

jigsawed letter

1x2

scrap 2x3

½ dowels from roll top desk

garden stakes, scraps

scrap wainscotting

scrap plywood

and Sheetrock. Renovation-site Dumpsters are great for finding odd bits of molding, trims, floorboards, wood with a little character, and sometimes larger architectural pieces like doors, banisters, decorative plaster chunks, or rabbeted lintels. You may also find a piece of broken furniture that has interesting wood to salvage, for example the segmented linen-backed sliding covers of a rolltop desk (the thin vertical strips, opposite), coffee table legs, louvers from shutters, or wooden gutters. Once the basic mantel is put together you can add details, like the W and M initials we jigsawed from a scrap piece of wood and glued on (opposite), or the lighted Wary Meyers logo above the initials (see Lightbox, page 108). Unfortunately we can't tell you how to make a Murphy bed, but at least this give you a jumping-off point.

To make something like the mantel on the previous page, you'll need to pull together all your scrap wood. (If you're finding the scrap gathering not lucrative for big flat surfaces, sometimes it's cost effective to go buy a 4"x8' sheet of plywood at the lumberyard; there is no shame in a 95% recycled mantel.)

The first step is designing it. We put together some sketches of ideas; some are kind of basic, some are odd. The more you sketch out concepts, the more concepts will come to you, and if you sketch long enough they'll become so conceptual as to not be practical (I'm not sure how either the snail or Lord Mayor's hand could be worked in). But then some conceptual ideas could make the greatest fireplace ever (the traditional silhouette with a pair of Staffordshire dogs).

step 1

Figure out how high you want the mantel to be. An easy height is 4'; since this is a common length for lumber it won't involve a lot of cutting and measuring. Cut eight pieces of 2x4" to 48". Cut the covering pieces out of plywood: four pieces at 10x48", and four pieces at 12x48". Lay down two pieces of 48" 2x4" and screw on the 12x48", as shown in the diagram. Make the 12x48" pieces first, then screw the fronts on, then the backs. You may choose to not have a piece on the back, as it'll be up against a wall and not visible.

step 2

You now have two columns. Cut two more pieces of plywood to 12x48". This will be the horizontal mantel face and the top. Lay down the column and screw the face on (at the top of the column, naturally), then lift the connected columns upright and screw on the top. Now you have a basic mantle shape. You could finish the back between the columns, but you'll have to cut the plywood to fit in between the plywood of the columns, or else you'll have a gap when you push it against the wall. The underside of the horizontal mantel is optional, but easily made. Measure the width between the columns (it should be about 27") and cut that length. The depth is 12". The easiest way to connect that is to screw two strips of scrap 12"-long 1x2"s to the columns, front to back, and then screw the bottom onto this shape.

step 3

Start putting the decorative pieces on: these could be random scraps from anywhere, but if you plan on leaving the wood unfinished, make sure they all tie in together, and there are no standouts, like one piece that's been painted red, or a piece of MDF (Medium-density Fibreboard), or masonite, for example. We started with a big piece over the top, which hung over the sides by about an inch, and that seemed on par with a traditional mantel. Onto that we put some strip molding, and we cut this on a 45° angle so the corners would fit in a not-so-haphazard way. You could use a miter saw to cut that, but we just eyeballed it, as we didn't need to get it right in only one cut.

step 4

The bottoms of the columns are covered in bead board, or wainscoting, which is a nice wood to come across because of its grooved pattern, making your detail work easier. Above the wainscoting are some random pieces cut and nailed on in a random way. If you cut one length to 10" and one to 9", you'll create more highlights and shadows, making it seem like there are more details in the trimmings.

Above those pieces are the strips from a rolltop desk. Each piece was sliced from the linen back and nailed on with finishing nails. The strips were made of oak, a hard wood requiring pilot holes to prevent the nail from splitting it. We kept the strips to the front of the mantel to avoid it looking like a Corinthian column, and traditionally mantels generally confine the decoration to the faces.

step 5

The W and M are the details that make this personalized as well as custom. We drew the letter on a scrap piece of pine, and used a hand jigsaw to cut it out, twice, since the M is just the W turned 180°. This is a lucky break that helps maintain a symmetrical design. The bulky piece below the lintel is a piece of banister, with a piece of picture frame below that.

step 6

The middle of the lintel has our logo cut out by jigsaw, and lit from within through a piece of white Plexiglas. If you wanted to tread these ostentatious waters, see the Lightbox project (page 108), otherwise push the mantel against the wall and enjoy!

Faux Fireplaces.

1×3
1×2

cut

warymeyers

w/ staffordshire dog

traditional shape
cut into wall.
Nice as room divider
also

old beam

cut out

out

K

existing fireplace w/
new semicircle

radiator
covers

Fireplace

of course these are just points of departure.

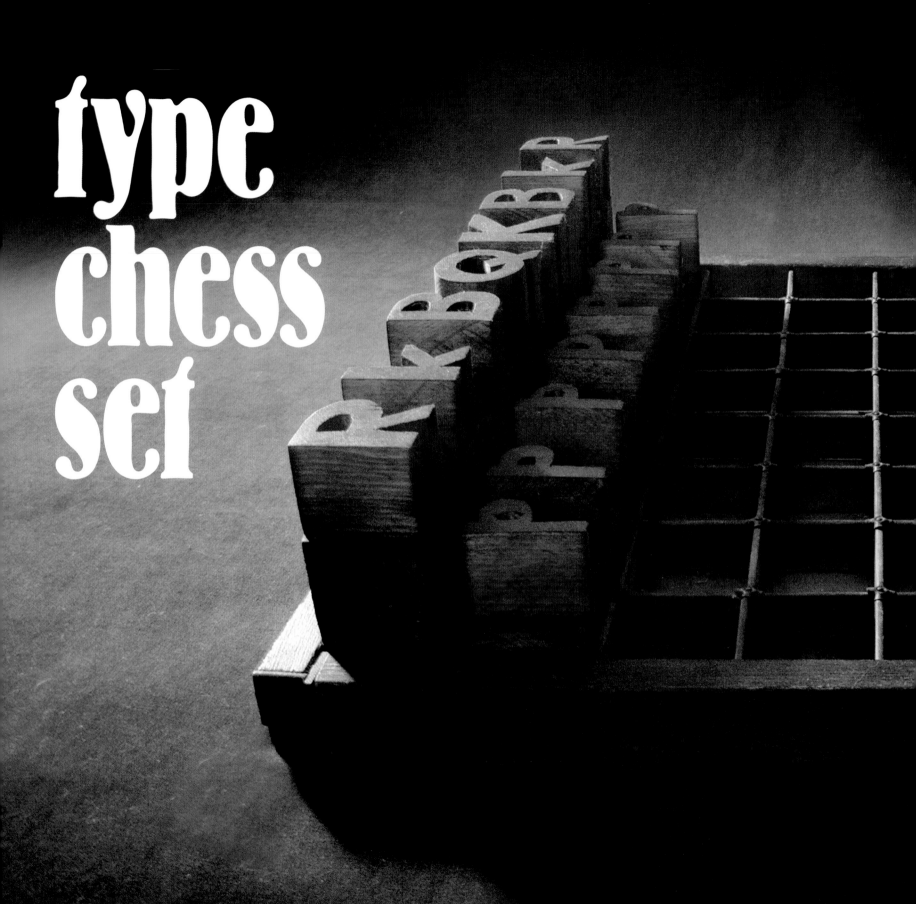

type
chess
set

Typography, the scroll saw, and boxes are three things we like to design with the most. Occasionally we'll think of something that could incorporate one of these or two, but one day at a garage sale the hat trick was presented to us in the form of an old type tray. Normally we don't really look twice at these, as I picture them hanging on a wall with a sprig of wheat and a thimble collection, but I've never noticed one that was laid out in an even grid like this. Also we'd been wanting to make a game of some kind. So this chess set came to mind. Our first thought was to use a block riser with some new design of the chess pieces on top of those, like an army of Jens Quistgaard teak pepper grinders rising on a battlefield. That would have been interesting, but then why bother with a type tray? The best design would be to use what's already there, or would be there, and just change one element of its own design. So that thinking brought us to this: blocks of type with the chess pieces represented by their first letter and colored, like old wood block type, by the residue of ink left on top of the type.

A few minor problems, like the repeated Ks of king and knight, were fixed by using upper- and lowercase type. The height of the pawns was kept lower, as is the case in a standard chess set. Chess is laid out on an 8x8" grid, so first you'll need to find an old type tray that has that, or at least a 7x7" grid. Unfortunately if your tray is anything but 8x8" you're in for quite a project as the craftsmanship of the 19th century was definitely built to last. These trays are made with pegs on each corner, thin nails at each cross of the segments, veneered bottoms hiding more nails inside, and everything seems connected, so there's a domino effect once you get one side apart. Do your best.

This is not an easy project, with 32 little letters to scroll saw, 30 center holes to saw, 48 blocks to cut, then the gluing, clamping, staining, and painting. To us it was well worth the effort, as the trinity of type, saw, and box came together. Looking at this photo, I picture the ghosts of Herb Lubalin on one side and Lou Dorfsman on the other, about to play a friendly game of

tools & supplies

- scrap wood 2x4"s, 2x6"s
- pencil
- drill
- ¼" bit
- scroll saw
- sandpaper
- needle files
- chop saw
- wood glue
- clamps
- wood stain
- black and white oil paint

Type

K (king)-2
Q (queen)-2
B (bishop)-4
k (knight)-4
R (rook)-4
p (pawn)-16

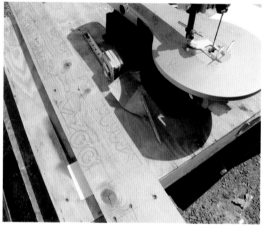

step 1

We used scrap 2x4"s and a 2x6" to cut the letters from. First, take the inside measurements of a section of the type tray. Ours measured 2" square, so we made a grid on the scrap wood of 1⅞" squares. Inside those we drew our letters. You can draw any type you want, but a sans serif is easiest and has the most impact; it's relatively anonymous and you want the set as a whole to be the design, not the fancy font. Plus when you look at the "board" you see the grid, and a sans serif flows nicely into a grid.

step 2

Once the pieces are drawn, drill a ¼" hole through each of the closed-looped letters (all but the Ks). Now cut out all the letters. Be slow and deliberate with the scroll saw, lest you break a blade. Try to keep as big a piece as you can, meaning don't cut each letter out right away—the longer they're connected, the easier it is to handle them, and this keeps your hands farther away from the blade. Cut out the loops at this time as well. We found the speed dial on the scroll saw to be a great help. Once the letters are all cut out, use sandpaper and needle files (these help inside the loops) to make them as perfect as you can.

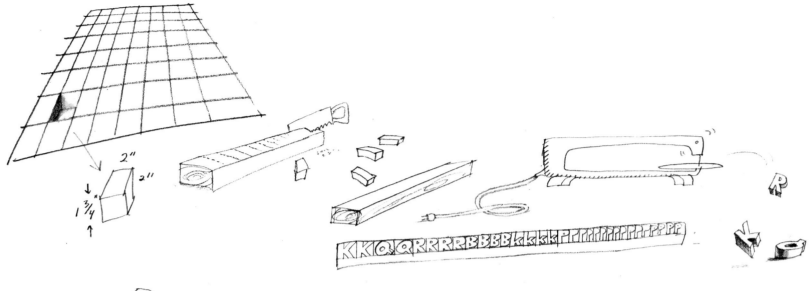

step 3

You also need to cut out the bases for the letters. Scrap 2x4"s are only 1¾" thick, so we couldn't cut our bases lengthwise since we needed 1⅞". That means that the back row pieces would need to be made of bases that were doubled up. Make a grid again just like the one made for the letters, and saw the blocks out. This is easiest with a chop saw. Make sure all the pieces are the same size, or very close. Cut 48 blocks. Set aside 16 for the pawns and wood glue the rest together, to make a block twice the height of the pawn blocks. These you'll need to clamp as the glue dries.

step 4

Once the blocks are set, sand all the sides to make them as smooth as possible, especially on the cross-cut sides. Use wood glue to glue the letters on. There's no need to clamp them, as you may inadvertently break a letter or smear the glue. However, do make sure the letters are all squared with the sides of the blocks. We put ours left-justified, with about ⅛" of kerning.

step 5

Once the glue dries on the letters you can stain them. We mixed up a dark walnut and chestnut, which we had laying around, but we suggest taking the type tray to the hardware store and matching a stain there. After the stain is dry paint the tops with a black oil paint, mixed with a tiny drop of violet, and a titanium white. Paint all the tops, wipe them off, and repaint them a few times, to achieve a kind of used look.

Linda and John Meyers are artists & designers. In 2004 they moved from New York City to Maine, married, and formed Wary Meyers Decorative Arts where they create a variety of artistic endeavors including paintings, interiors, illustration, design, and soft sculpture. Before Wary Meyers, Linda was a graphic designer and art director and John was the Corporate Display Director for Anthropologie.

Their work has been featured in multiple national and international publications, as well as the Portland Museum of Art. This is their first book.